Dedicated to those with Stress and Strain:

Walk your talk...

Run your fun

Printed and Bound by: Gilliland Printing, Inc.

Digital Proofs provided by: Advanced Digital Imaging, Inc.

Layout and Design by: Chris Silva

Acknowledgments of previously printed materials may be found at the end of this book.

Publisher's cataloging — in publication

Fahlman, Clyde
Laughing Nine to Five: The Quest for Humor in the Workplace/
by Clyde Fahlman
p. cm.
Includes bibliographical references and index
Preassigned LCCN: 97-91442
ISBN 0-9656055-3-1

1. Business Communication. 2. Humor in business.
3. Communication in management. I. Title

HF5718.F34 1997   658.4"5
                         QBI97-40265

Laughing
Nine to Five

The Quest for Humor in the Workplace

Clyde Fahlman

Preface

There are more standup comics then there have ever been. People actually make a living as humor consultants. College courses in humor have made humorology a legitimate, almost respectable, field of study.

Paradoxically, in the world of work, less humor exists.

There are a few workplace organizations where humor exists and is encouraged. They are led by people who care about people. (I will give examples and name names.)

But for many of us, where has the humor gone? It existed once. It was not a scarce resource. In the past ten years it has trickled to nothing or gone underground.

Why the change?

Here are the answers from the workplace, participants in management classes and workshops:

1. There isn't much to laugh about in most organizations. The job security issue is real. The threat or actuality of restructuring, reengineering, and downsizing permeates many organizations. When it happens the workload for those still employed is staggering; we need to "do more with less" a cheer leading management says. Ex-employees released to pasture, as well as those retained, see themselves as commodities. Not fun.

2. Many managers have returned to the sweatshop mentality. "Humor and laughter are not productive," they say, ignoring all evidence to the contrary. This philosophy has always existed, but with today's spin of the economy, it is returning as the default management style.

3. There exists now an element of political correctness that has made almost all humor suspect. Undeniably there is a requirement for sexual harassment and cultural diversity training. In those areas as well as others, the use of humor to hurt anyone is never appropriate; this will be

addressed later. This being said, however, it appears that people are discarding the natural situational humor as well as the harmful; they and their managements are confused as to what is normal and acceptable.

This sounds desperate.

It is.

Unquestionably, a book is a requirement for you to recapture humor for connection and perspective. I suggest this book. (Although worthy, I do not share in the royalties of other books.)

Now to something equally important:

My wife Dorothy has put up with my mumbling and musings for years; she has been more supportive than I deserve. Admittedly, she has advised our children to avoid me when I get on a Tom Swiftie roll (something I do happily in a later niche in this book). However, she has stood by me, watching me turn into a mellowed curmudgeon.

There are others. All the students in my management classes and workshops have, with their collective contributions, raised my humor consciousness to new levels. Included in this book are the offerings, the funny and thought provoking offerings of workshop participants Ginger Abel, Suzy Bicknese, Kacie Christie, Erin Davis, Carol L. Doane, Kelly Foutts-Smith, Jeanine Hickman, John McCauley, Lori Medak, Pat Ross, Lou Schmerber, Jodi Syverson, and Rashelle Turner. Many thanks as well to illustrator John Haugse and designer Chris Silva for their most creative efforts.

I am also very appreciative of the superb editorial and overall support by Linny and Dennis Stovall. This tome would never have made it to the shelves without them. They, and all those listed above, should be held blameless for the tangents, the crazies, and any mistakes. Those belong to me.

If there is any doubt, I must make it clear that this book is written for you. If someone in top management uses it as a tool for improving the climate of the office or operation, this is clearly a bonus. (Realizing, however, that it is highly unlikely that your higher management will reimburse you for the purchase of this book, I have decided not to make a big play for their support.)

Chapter One

In the Beginning: You

Congratulations!

You are funny. There is supporting evidence to verify that you have the seventh sense of humor. Everyone in your organization knows it. There is no need for denial.

I have also learned from people, just like you, who have attended our workshops. They at first said they didn't have a sense of humor, only to learn that they were very funny and could see the humor in everything. (If you are ever in the area I might be able to get you a good deal on the price of a workshop.)

That means you have an advantage. You know that humor plays a significant role in the reduction of stress, improved work performance and communication, increased creativity, and the maintenance and betterment of personal health. Positive humor builds connection and develops perspective. It is conceivable that it even improves the mysterious "bottom line."

Today's work world is tension filled. Hourly wages and monthly salaries are stagnant and the amount of expected work is up. Employees are desperate. With the phenomena of deloading, right sizing, outsourcing, and other new clichés, work environments are not user friendly. There are things you can do to relieve this stress such as get rest, watch your diet, and exercise, but you need comic relief as well.

This book is for you. I do not dislike your middle or top management. There are worse organizations than the one where you work. I might even agree with your management when they say or infer: "Trust us." However, in a face-off between you and your organization you have to be aware I would be behind you every time. It is your humor well-being that counts. (Of course if you become a humor asset, your organization might benefit as well.)

I can remember you when you were a small child.

Perhaps that is when you had some first doubts about humor. You were once heard to say that you didn't have a funny bone in your body.

Why this doubt?

Most likely your humor was suppressed at an early age, maybe shortly before or after graduation from your real cut and paste days, about age five or six. It occurred about the same time that creativity was discouraged. Some authority figure in your life said, "That's a nice picture, but now it's time to do something practical like count to two hundred." (In fairness to your parents, there may not have been any more room on the refrigerator door for additional drawings.)

There were other directive comments that prompted you to abandon humor:

"WHAT'S SO FUNNY?" ("NOTHING. NOTHING. YOU HAVE LETTUCE ON YOUR CHIN AND I'M NOT GOING TO TELL YOU.")

"IF THAT'S SO FUNNY, DO YOU WANT TO SHARE IT WITH US?" (TEACHERS AND PARENTS NEED TO CONTROL THINGS.)

"WIPE THAT SMILE OFF YOUR FACE." ("WILL I GET THAT ON MY SLEEVE TOO?")

"THAT'S NOT VERY FUNNY." (THIS IS WHEN WE LEARNED THAT HUMOR COULD BE GRADED AND THEREFORE WAS HIGH-RISK STUFF.)

"WHAT HAVE YOU DONE NOW?" ("NOTHING. NOTHING I WANT TO SHARE WITH YOU. I'M SICK OF TIME-OUTS IN THE CORNER.")

"YOU'RE DISTURBING THE CLASS." (THEY NEEDED A WAKEUP CALL.)

"GET SERIOUS." (THIS HAS THE OBVIOUS IMPLICATION THAT HUMOR HAS NOTHING TO DO WITH THE HUMAN CONDITION IN THE REAL WORLD.)

"I DON'T KNOW WHY YOU CAN'T BE MORE LIKE YOUR OLDER SISTER. SHE ACTS GROWN UP." (THIS WAS THE FIRST TIME WE LEARNED SHE WAS SOMEONE TO WATCH OUT FOR.)

"MOM, HE'S MAKING FUN OF ME." ("I DIDN'T TEASE HER. BESIDES, SHE DESERVED IT.")

"JOHN, MAYBE YOU CAN TELL US WHAT IS SO INTERESTING OUT THAT WINDOW?" (SO WENT THE VISION OF YOUR LEADING A GROUP OF NBA ALL-STARS IN SLAM DUNKS.)

"STOP THAT LAUGHING. YOU'RE GOING TO BE CRYING PRETTY SOON." (TO THIS DAY DO YOU UNDERSTAND THE CONNECTION?)

These kinds of memories will help you reexamine the humor in your life. In addition to your parents (your first supervisors), there were Uncle Fred and one of your grandfathers. (Grandpa Rex was a character, telling it as it was. Remember? He was the one who walked to school three miles each day through the snow—"uphill both ways.") In spite of admonitions to become more serious, you were saved many times by funny people around you. You only need to recall them.

More You

Consider your place in the family. If you were the oldest child you were obligated to help your parents. With no experience your parents needed someone with which to practice. That was you. There was no time for humor, particularly later when you became a role model. Fortunately you learned to be a list maker. Today you can do something about humor. Simply put it on your daily to do list. (If you do not pre-pare such lists, you should ask your parents if you really were the first child.) Treat it as any other item on the list. You can only cross out your humor entry by exhibiting it in some fashion.

If you were the middle child you played off the oldest, having more friends and the ability to laugh at almost everything, including having the fewest pictures in the family album. A case could be made for mid-dle children having more humor genes than anyone else.

Being the youngest was cool. You were the entertainer playing off everyone. You learned how to handle permissive (read tired) parents. You were cute at the same time you were funny and totally unappreciat-ed by older siblings.

Even today, when your entire family gets together it's possible these roles are maintained with little modification. When this happens see the cup as half full and laugh.

Get in touch with the kinds of things that trigger your laughter: sit-coms (maybe) and movies (maybe) but perhaps even more, situational spontaneous humor. The greatest practitioners of spontaneous humor include two and three year olds, the antics of inquisitive squirrels and monkeys, and people who dress for success. (Not to be slighted is human interaction with dogs and/or cats.)

The next step in your humor trace is for you to come up with at least two funny things about yourself.

Think of events in your life:

- THE ATTRACTIVE BOY (GIRL) IN THE SEAT NEXT TO YOU IN THE SEVENTH GRADE AND WHAT YOU DID TO IMPRESS HIM OR HER.

- A LITTLE LEAGUE BASEBALL GAME OR JUNIOR HIGH BASKETBALL GAME THAT SAW ONE OF YOUR PARENTS EVICTED FOR YELLING AT AN OFFICIAL.

- CHAPERONING OR BABY-SITTING YOUNGER CHILDREN IN THE FAMILY. (YOU WERE BLAMED, REMEMBER, BECAUSE AT YOUR AGE "YOU SHOULD KNOW BETTER.")

- OUTDOOR SCHOOL. (YOU BECAME HOMESICK OR JUST PLAIN SICK.)

- THE PROM. (YOUR DATE GOT SICK.)

- A SKIP DAY THAT WASN'T AUTHORIZED, AND YOUR FOLKS FOUND OUT ABOUT IT.

- YOUR FIRST DATE. (YOUR ZITS WERE AT THEIR ZENITH.)

- LEARNING TO DRIVE WITH YOUR PARENT NEAR APOPLEXY AND YOUR FAILURE TO PUT LIFE PRESERVING THINGS IN THE CAR LIKE OIL AND ANTIFREEZE.

- GAMES YOU WON, LEGITIMATELY AND OTHERWISE, WITH SIBLINGS.

- THE SWIMMING SUIT YOU LOST IN THE WATER AFTER A FANTASTIC DIVE.

- A STRANGE DREAM. (YOU RESCUED SOMEONE WHO COULDN'T STAND YOU—BEFORE OR AFTER. YOU STILL HAD ZITS.)

- YOUR CAT. (SHE DEMANDED MILK AT 4:05 A.M. EVERY DAY)

- A STRANGE GIFT. (YOU RECEIVED A RAKE FOR YOUR ROOM FROM YOUR PARENTS.)

- YOUR FIRST DAY ON THE JOB. (YOU WORE SHOES THAT DIDN'T MATCH, BUT THEY WERE BOTH THE SAME COLOR.)

- THE BIGGEST MISTAKE YOU EVER MADE. (YOU REAR ENDED THE BOSS'S WIFE-THAT IS HER CAR-AND TOLD OTHERS SHE WAS AT FAULT. LATER YOU FOUND OUT WHO SHE WAS.)

- YOUR SKIRT FELL OFF IN FRONT OF THE COKE MACHINE.

- FOUR PEOPLE FAINTED AT YOUR WEDDING.

Okay, you have it. There are many funny things about yourself. Some are in your own memory hard drive. Recover those files to help you and those around you at work.

You are not the first I've asked to do this.

Others Find Their Humor

With only minimal coaxing, participants in humor workshops have reconstructed their humor histories, contributing the following funny things about themselves.

Here is what they discovered:

"I WILL RUN THREE TO FOUR MILES A DAY FOR WEIGHT CONTROL AND THEN EAT A HALF DOZEN CHOCOLATE DOUGHNUTS AT A SINGLE SEATING."

"MY HUSBAND INTRODUCES ME AS HIS FIRST WIFE."

"WHEN I COMMUNICATE AT WORK I'VE BEEN KNOWN TO BE SO INDIRECT THAT PEOPLE HAVE SEPARATE MEETINGS LATER TO DETERMINE WHAT I SAID."

"MY COMPUTER GOES THROUGH LONG PERIODS OF SILENCE WHEN IT SEES MY SPELLING."

"DESPITE THE FACT THAT I HAVE TOO MANY UNDERWEAR IN MY DRAWERS, I DON'T THROW OUT THE ONE WITH HOLES." (WHAT'S SO FUNNY ABOUT THAT?)

"I SMOKE ON THE WAY TO THE HEALTH CLUB."

"I INVENT NEW WORDS. PEOPLE SEEM TO KNOW WHAT THEY MEAN."

"I FINISH MY HUSBAND'S SENTENCES FOR HIM, THEN I TELL HIM HE'S WRONG."

"I TALK SLOW AND THINK FASTER. I END UP TALKING IN PHRASES THAT DON'T TIE TOGETHER AND/OR MAKE SENSE."

"WHEN I OPERATE A MACHINE I MAKE A MOTOR NOISE."

"WHEN I'M IN A HURRY I PULL MY PANTY HOSE UP CROOKED. SURE MAKES ME WALK FUNNY."

"I GO AROUND AND PUSH CHAIRS UP CLOSE TO TABLES WHICH CO-WORKERS FIND HILARIOUS. THEY LEAVE THEM OUT ON PURPOSE."

"I HAVE FIGURED HOW TO LIVE ON POVERTY LEVEL INCOME WHILE ACCUMU-LATING A SAVING ACCOUNT MOST WOULD BE PROUD OF. NOW I CAN'T BRING MYSELF TO SPEND IT."

"THE DOG AND I LAUGH AT EACH OTHER WHEN I COME HOME FROM WORK. REALLY."

"I DRAW PICTURES FOR ALMOST ALL EXPLANATIONS. PEOPLE LAUGH WHEN I CAN'T FIND A PENCIL OR PAPER."

"I HATE BEING WET AND COLD, BUT I LOVE THE PACIFIC NORTHWEST."

"I LIKE TO RIDE MOTORCYCLES BUT PREFER TO RIDE WHEN MY NAILS ARE PAINTED RED."

"I ENJOY SEEING MY FORMER WIFE WORK IN HER GARDEN. TO HELP HER WITH HER GREEN THUMB I PUT LETTUCE SEED IN HER FRONT LAWN LATE AT NIGHT."

"PARKING LOTS. I GO IN ON THE OUT AND OUT ON THE IN."

"I ALWAYS TALK TO MYSELF, DEBATING ISSUES OUT LOUD. PEOPLE STOP TO HEAR THE OUTCOMES OF THIS TWO-WAY COMMUNICATION."

"I MANGLE VERSIONS OF POPULAR SONG LYRICS, AND IT SEEMS TO IMPROVE THE SONGS."

"I TELL PEOPLE WHO SAY 'I'VE BEEN THINKING' NOT TO DO THAT ANYMORE."

"I HIT MY HUSBAND WITH A NEWSPAPER TO MAKE MY DOG BEHAVE."

"I TALK WITH MY CATS AND THEY ANSWER. THEY'RE ESPECIALLY GOOD WITH SARCASM."

When you are able to see the humor in yourself you have the vision to see it everywhere. The most important part of this process is the ability to laugh at yourself. A little self-effacing humor does a lot to open doors of communication and establish connection. If you can laugh at yourself, you have established a climate of openness. We then can feel comfortable "being human" and revealing the funny things about ourselves. Once again, we connect.

Perhaps one of the greatest practitioners at making light of himself was former president Ronald Reagan. At his seventieth birthday he said it was really the thirty-first anniversary of his thirty-ninth birthday. On his seventy-fifth birthday he added that seventy-five was really only twenty degrees Celsius. When entering the operating room after a gunman's attempted assassination, Reagan said he hoped that the surgeons were Republicans.

There are many potential self-effacing opportunities for you (for anyone) at work. Here is a possibility. When you are congratulated for a promotion by one of your peers here are a few suggested responses:

"NOW, I'LL BE ABLE TO CONTRIBUTE TO THE OFFICE CANDY DISH."

"I WONDER IF I STILL HAVE TO MOW THE BOSS'S LAWN."

"THEY MUST HAVE LOOKED AT SOMEONE ELSE'S RESUME."

"NOW I HAVE TO ACT LIKE I KNOW WHAT I'M DOING."

"I GUESS THIS IS IT. I WILL NEVER BE SELECTED AS EMPLOYEE OF THE MONTH."

"DO YOU THINK IT HELPS THAT MY SECOND COUSIN IS A VICE-PRESIDENT?"

"SOMETIMES YOU LUCK OUT WHEN YOU'RE HALF-WAY BETWEEN THE PETER PRINCIPLE AND THE DILBERT PRINCIPLE."

"WHO WOULD THINK A LOW HANDICAP IN GOLF WOULD BE OF THIS MUCH VALUE."

"TO BE FAIR THEY ALSO HAVE TO TAKE PEOPLE FROM THE UNQUALIFIED POOL."

"IT'S JUST ONE MORE EXAMPLE THAT TOP MANAGEMENT IS INFALLIBLE. WHAT WERE THEY THINKING OF?"

"I ALWAYS WANTED TO WRITE MEMOS."

"YOU SCREW UP—YOU MOVE UP."

""NOW I HAVE TO FAKE IT UNTIL I MAKE IT."

You can always laugh at yourself or the situation. For instance, if you were able to come up with a quick name that described you—maybe even the way you wanted to be—what would it be? River Rat? Sally Siren? Pole Cat? Working Fool? 007? Food Bandit? Macho? Sport? Groupie? Heartbreak? Figured? De-wrinkled? Intoxicating? Sparkle? Luring? Blurring? Inspiring? Perspiring Pal?

Do you have something in mind for yourself? Of course you do and it's very reasonable to share this name with yourself. The opportunity to see yourself in an entirely different light gives you a chance to see the many opportunities for humor around you. You could have a new name every month. (If your organization has new visions and new "flavors" periodically, why can't you have a new name?)

The Child's View

What do you think a child's view of your adult roles might be? Your children? The child in you?

Here are some possibilities:

"I WANT TO GO TO WORK AND PLAY COMPUTER GAMES ALL DAY LIKE THEY DO."

"MOMMY HAS TO WORK SOMETIMES. NO MONEY GROWS ON TREES."

"HIS JOB IS DUMB."

"SHE SITS AT A DESK WITH A PUTTER AND TALKS ON THE PHONE AND RUNS AROUND ALL OVER."

"MY DADDY WORKS IN A TALL BUILDING. THEY DON'T LET HIM OUT UNTIL AFTER BEDTIME."

"THEY BRING WORK HOME AT NIGHT AND PUT SHEETS OF PAPER INTO PILES."

"SOMEDAY I'M GOING TO WORK WITH MY DADDY TO SEE THE CLOWNS HE WORKS WITH."

"THEY HATE SOMETHING CALLED THE BOSS. I THINK IT HAS SOMETHING TO DO WITH WHITE AND BROWN COWS."

"I WISH MY MOM WOULDN'T BRING SO MUCH WORK HOME. COULDN'T THEY JUST PUT HER INTO A SLOWER LEARNING GROUP?"

"THEY HAVE CHAIRS WITH WHEELS ON THEM."

"ONLY AFTER THEY DRINK THEIR 'MORNING COFFEE' DO THEY TALK TO US."

"THEIR COMPUTERS MUST BE BAD DRIVERS BECAUSE THEY CRASH."

"THEY MUST HAVE A LOT OF 'TIME OUTS' AT WORK."

"WHEN I CALL THEM AT WORK THEY WHISPER SO I CAN'T HEAR THEM."

"I DON'T THINK THEY WOULD HAVE MUCH TO SAY AT SHOW AND TELL."

"ALL THEY DO AT RECESS IS DRINK COFFEE."

"DO YOU THINK THEY'RE POOPED?"

"IF WE HAD STAIRS THAT MOVED WE COULD HAVE FUN TOO."

"THEY CAN ONLY BE LATE COMING HOME FROM WORK."

"THE ROAD FROM WORK MUST BE BUMPY, MAMA'S TIRED AND DADDY'S GRUMPY."

"I LIKE SATURDAYS BECAUSE MOM TAKES ME TO WHERE SHE WORKS AND I CAN TAKE PICTURES OF MY HANDS."

"IN THE AFTERNOON SHE TAKES A NAP AND THEN GOES HOME AFTER SNACK TIME."

"DID YOU KNOW MY MOMMY WORKS FOR A WITCH?"

Here is a very useful exercise: Devote five minutes a day to thinking what your child, grandchild, or you as a child would have said about those awfully important things you did yesterday.

Try these:

I had a meeting with a high level human resources director who could have an impact on my future. Your child might say: "I wish Daddy drove a cement truck."

I listened to an attorney talk about potential damages in some of our transactions. "Daddy often takes naps in the afternoon. At work they wake him up so he can come home."

If I play my cards right I may have an opportunity to be promoted and make substantially more money. "I don't understand why daddy doesn't play cards with me anymore."

They say all the right things but I'm not sure there really is an opportunity for women in this business. "Mommy, why do I have to wear a dress at your Christmas party?"

Random Thoughts

Think of the random thoughts that race back and forth in your ever active brain. In several workshop sessions participants were asked to record their thoughts about anything and everything. Here is a composite list of what they were thinking about:

"This is dumb... I wish I had a computer... I wish I had a large cold drink and I don't mean a Pepsi... I want to win the lottery... Is this guy for real... Should I get a second job... How can I get along with my sister... My back hurts... Boy am I tired... I hate writing... I wonder if George is putting Windows in the computer. Will it be done this century? George Junior is just like him...Wonder if I can make phone calls during the break.

"John is a real pain in the butt... It's a good thing this is anonymous, because if I wrote down what I am thinking it would be more than embarrassing... Why am I only writing about vacuuming and cleaning the house... Wonder if the dogs have broken through the screen door... Some people are not willing to let go of the past... This instructor is weird... Got this sweater from Victoria's Secret... My fingernail broke. Why tonight... I'm starving... I wish I weighed one hundred and twenty with the appropriate body sculpted measurements... I wonder if Jake will call tonight... What's for dinner...

"How can I get out of being pre-labeled, because of my supervisor's action... I've got to go to the bathroom... The kids will probably drive me nuts... I guess I can't worry about my peers or manager... I just wore a sweater in here... I'm going to freeze my butt off going to the

car... Hope my daughter and family are gone from my house tonight...
This chair is really hard... I hope this stuff will apply to all... I guess I
can't worry about my peers or managers... Why am I doing this silly ass
assignment?"

And more:

"Get gas on way home... hope to hear from son in Las Vegas... need
to back up computer files tomorrow... my pen stopped working... I'm
cold and I miss by wife... Do I have enough money to eat out... I don't
really think I've been asked to write down random thoughts before so I
guess I shouldn't be surprised if I kind of muck around. What to wear
there? When will the title come. My stomach is hurting."

*Look at that last paragraph as if you were your mother. What
would she say?*

Here is a possibility: "I certainly hope you don't run out of gas...
you never planned ahead... I remember in high school we had to go
pick you up for the same reason... I don't know why you ever let your
son go to Las Vegas anyway... You should always have two pens with
you... If you were a little closer I could fix dinner for you. I don't
understand why your wife doesn't cook a casserole for you when she has
to be out of town... I don't know why this exercise should be so difficult
for you... you were always daydreaming and, your stomach wouldn't
hurt if you just ate right."

Okay. Here is the last chance for more random thoughts.

"Work load is really bothering me. Wish this chair was more comfortable. I want to succeed in my educational endeavors without burn-
ing myself out. At seven hundred parts repaired the boss will meet his
goal of one thousand repaired panels from my department and hopefully
that means no Saturday work. I need to go shopping. "

*This time re-do the previous paragraph as if a boss were comment-
ing on your thoughts:*

"When I was your age I had twice as much work and got it done in the evening if I had to. I am sure your chair is ergonomically sound. I too hope you don't spend too much time on your night school and get tired out during the day. Do they ever teach you anything of practical value over there? It really is about time we started getting the thousand parts. In my day we worked Saturdays all the time and were really glad to get all the overtime. I would appreciate it if you didn't make out your shopping lists here at work. Others don't know you are on a break".

Now tell me one more time. Aren't you funny? Aren't we all?

This is a worthwhile five minute exercise for getting in touch with yourself. Try it.

Struggling With Ego

The Scottish poet Robert Burns said it well:

"O what some power be given us,
To see ourselves as others see us!
It would from many a blunder free us..."

Many people can't get beyond their egos. An obsession with the importance of self is funny, but it can turn out to be devastating if you don't get it. There are a group of people out there dubbed "Type A" that really do not get it.

Here are their attributes:

You (Sorry. We mean "they") schedule more activities into less and less time. (They put too much garbage in and the sack breaks.)

They hurry the speech of others. (They feelthebestwheneverythin-grunstogether.)

They get angry at people driving too slow. (If you are in a parking lot it makes good sense to let them get out first.)

They hate to wait in line. (At a grocery store they will report someone in the express lane who has more than eight items in their shopping basket.)

They are always on time. (They cut people off in conversations, get speeding tickets, take short cuts, and are never fashionably late; meetings must start without small talk. They are upset when others show up more than a minute late.)

They have difficulty sitting and doing nothing. (They simply do not understand the essence of most staff jobs.)

They become impatient when watching others do things. (They were promoted because they did that same thing so well. They never got over it.)

They are finger tappers and doodle to excess in meetings.

If you know someone like this (maybe real well) tell them to stand on a chair next to the lamp in the ceiling. (See # ten below.)

Further, if you (or that other person) have any of the tendencies discussed above. here's a useful list of things to get back on track:

1. SEEK OUT CARTOONS—PARTICULARLY THOSE ABOUT WORK. (THERE ARE WORLD-QUALITY CARTOONS LIKE DILBERT.)

2. LOOK FOR COMEDY ANYWHERE: VIDEOS, MOVIES, SIT-COMS-EVEN BOOKS LIKE THIS ONE. (IN FACT I SUGGEST YOU BUY THIS BOOK FOR EVERY CO-WORKER AND ALL OF YOUR RELATIVES. SEND ONE TO A FRIEND IN THE FAR EAST. NEW YORK? NEW MARKETS FOR BOOKS ARE OPENING UP THERE. THERE IS NO REASON WHY THIS BOOK SHOULD NOT BE TRANS-LATED INTO CHINESE OR BULGARIAN. THE PUBLISHER HAS ASKED THAT I INCLUDE A LITTLE MARKETING MATERIAL IN THE BOOK.)

3. WHEN STRESSED, ASK IF ANYONE IN ICELAND CARES. (PERHAPS THIS IS TOO STRONG. YOU MAY ACTUALLY KNOW SOMEONE THERE. THE QUESTION STILL REMAINS, HOWEVER: DO THEY CARE?)

4. LAUGH LOUDLY WITH CO-WORKERS. (HAVING HEARD THE EXPRESSION "CRYING OUT LOUD," THERE IS A NEED TO CONSIDER "LAUGHING OUT LOUD.")

5. YES. LAUGH IF SOMETHING IS FUNNY, EVEN IF YOU ARE ALONE WITH YOUR CAT. (IF YOUR CAT IS WITH YOU AT WORK YOU MAY HAVE TO EXPLAIN THAT TO SOMEONE. IF YOU ARE TELECOMMUTING YOU WILL NOT. IF YOUR WORK AREA IS BEING MONITORED BY SECURITY YOU MAY HAVE TO SMILE TO YOURSELF.)

6. SPONTANEOUSLY LOOK FOR THE FUNNY SIDE. (SEE CHAPTER ON FORMU-LAS. ALSO YOU CAN LOOK FOR THE FUNNY SIDE WITHOUT BEING SPONTA-NEOUS.)

7. SEND HUMOROUS NOTES, BOOKS, AND CALENDARS TO FRIENDS WHO SHOULD PURGE STRESS AND TENSION.

8. DEVELOP LAUGH LINES AROUND YOUR EYES. (YOU ARE GOING TO DEVEL-OP FACIAL LINES ANYWAY SO THEY MIGHT AS WELL TELL A GOOD STORY.)

9. BE SURE TO BRUSH AFTER EVERY MEAL. (WE WILL BE LOOKING AT YOUR TEETH WHEN YOU SMILE.)

10. STAND ON A CHAIR NEXT TO THE FIXTURE IN THE CEILING? YES. LIGHTEN UP.

In summary: You are funny. It's time to re-discover this. Everything about you, around you, is funny. If you are still not sure, examine the list of potential irritants in Figure 1. Seeing them in perspective, you'll find them humorous.

Figure 1

Irritants That Incite	...Something Worse?
Spreadsheets	Empty toilet roll
People you know but can't place	Being on hold
Machines that eat money	Credit cards that eat money
Someone who says "Got a minute?"	Time management
Printers that fade	Copiers that jam

Rest rooms with no doors	The expression "my door is always open"
Writing employee evaluations	Receiving evaluations
People who say yes and mean no	An ex-wife and her attorney
Buttons that fall off	Needle holes too small to thread
Slow driver in fast lane	Fast driver with car phone
Temporary work	Too many trips to rest room
Voice mail with too many options	Unsolicited calls
Cars that tailgate	People who tailgate
People who don't smile at you when you smile at them	People who smile at you and blame you

Chapter Two

Laughter: For Your Health

We can't leave the subject of "you" without talking about your health.

There are mine fields out there ready to do real damage to you, your body, and your mind. Here is but one: It is likely that you will have three to five career changes and ten job changes in your lifetime. Many of them will be involuntary. To say the least this makes for stress which can have ill effects on your health.

Face it. Say good-bye to cradle to grave employment with one employer. (Actually the concept and the practice of life time work with one employer is kind of boring anyway.) Anticipate it and keep your perspective.

There is a good chance that you will find employment with the fastest growing industry in the country: Temporary (yes with a big t) employers. Look at it this way: You can help the economy and make it possible for many organizations to benefit from your sense of humor. If you can laugh about it—maybe even giggle—you have a good chance of staying healthy.

It is highly unlikely that you will take my word for it.

But there is evidence.

Hippocrates, father of medicine, insisted that medical students give full weight to the emotions, both as a contributing cause of disease as well as a factor in recovery.

Medical researchers at many medical centers have been studying the effects of laughter on the human body and have discovered a wide array of beneficial changes, all the way from enhanced respiration to increases in the number of disease fighting immune cells.

Jane E. Brody, personal health column writer for the *New York Times* reports that laughter's impact on cardiovascular and respiratory functions are of particular note:

"When one is laughing hard, normal breathing rhythm is disrupted. Inhalation and expiration become more spasmodic as well as deeper. Heart rate, blood pressure, and muscular tension increase, but when laughter subsides, these levels often drop temporarily to below normal, leaving one very relaxed. Hence the expression 'weak with laughter' to describe someone who has just laughed hard and long.

"This sense of relaxation lasts about 45 minutes after the last laugh, and may be beneficial in countering heart disease, high blood pressure and depression. Given these benefits, proponents of laughter therapy jokingly call it 'ho-ho-holistic medicine.'

In his books, *Anatomy of an Illness* and *Head First,* Norman Cousins, the late author and lecturer, documented and publicized the importance of humor and laughter in reducing pain and improving health. His impact on the holistic view of medicine was considerable—more perhaps than any lay person before or since.

Cousins told his own story in the following excerpt from a magazine article:

> I walked into the meeting room at the Sepulveda (California) Veteran's Administration Hospital. As a member of the Department of Psychiatry and Bio-behavioral Sciences at the UCLA School of Medicine—work I began after my retirement as editor of the Saturday Review—I had frequently been asked by the dean and faculty members to visit patients who had given up the fight. My job was to restore hope, to show patients how they themselves could work with their doctors to relieve pain and enhance recovery. But this assignment, I could see, was going to be tough.
>
> The 50 or 60 veterans in the cancer unit sat in rows and were every bit as glum as I had anticipated. I told them their doctors were concerned about their mood and said I doubted that they were helping their physicians or themselves with the grim mood of the place. Certainly, one could understand the reason for their feelings—and it was arrogant for anyone to lecture them about it. But they were reaching out for help—and they were entitled to know what would optimize that prospect.
>
> Any battle with serious illness, I said, involved two elements. One was represented by the ability of the physicians to make available to patients the best that medical science has to offer. The other element was represented by the ability of patients to summon all their physical and spiritual resources in fighting illness. Their job, I hoped they'd agree, was to create an environment in which the doctors could do their best. I then suggested some ways they might replace the grim atmosphere—watch funny movies or listen to tapes of stand-up comics.

I was speaking from firsthand experience. Many years ago I was hobbled by a disease of the connective tissue. At that time I discovered that ten minutes of belly laughter would give me two hours of pain-free sleep. Since my illness involved severe inflammation of the spine and joints, making it painful even to turn over in bed, the practical value of laughter became a significant feature of treatment.

William Hitzig, MD, my physician, was as fascinated as I was by the clear evidence that laughter could be a potent painkiller. He tested this proposition by comparing my sedimentation rate—which measures the extent of inflammation or infection in the body—both before and after my response to amusing situations in films or books. Since my sedimentation rate was in the upper range, any reduction was to be welcomed. Dr. Hitzig reported to me that just a few moments of robust laughter had knocked a significant number of units off the sedimentation rate. Most interesting was that the reduction held and was cumulative.

The veterans accepted the challenge. When I returned to the hospital several weeks later the doctors described the change in the general environment and in the mood of the individual patients. Each person was obligated to tell of something good that had happened to him since the previous meeting.

The first veteran spoke of his success in reaching a buddy he had not seen since the Korean War. The next veteran read from a letter he had received from a nephew who had just been admitted to medical school "Uncle Ben, I want you to know that I'm going into cancer research, and I'm going to come up with the answer, so just hang in there until I do."

Cheers.

And so it went, each person taking his turn Then I discovered that everyone was looking at me.

I searched my recent memory and realized that something good had in fact just happened to me.

"What I have to report is better than good," I began. "It's wonderful."

The veterans sat forward.

"'What happened is that when I arrived at the Los Angeles airport last Wednesday my bag was the first off the carousel."

An eruption of applause.

"I had never even met anyone whose bag was the first off the carousel," I continued. "Flushed with success, I went to the nearest telephone to report my arrival to my office. That was when I lost my coin...and I decided to report it to the operator."

"Operator," I said, "I put in a quarter and didn't get my number. The machine collected my coin."

"Sir," she said, "if you give me your name and address, we'll mail the coin to you." I was appalled.

"Operator," I said, "I think I can understand the reason behind the difficulties of AT&T. They're going to take the time and trouble to write down my name on a card and then you are probably going to give it to the person in charge of such matters. He will go to the cash register, punch it open and take out a quarter, at the same time recording the reason for the cash withdrawal. Then he will take a cardboard with a recessed slot to hold the coin so it won't flop around in the envelope. Then he, or someone else, will fit the cardboard with the coin into an envelope, first taking the time to write out my address on the envelope. Then the envelope will be sealed. Someone will then affix a stamp on the envelope. All that time and expense just to return a quarter. Now, operator, why don't you just return my coin and let's be friends."

"Sir," she repeated in a flat voice, "if you give me your name and address, we will mail you the refund."

Then, almost by way of after-thought, she said, "Sir, did you remember to press the coin-return plunger?"

Truth to tell, I had overlooked this nicety. I pressed the plunger. To my great surprise, all at once, the machine proceeded to spew out coins.

While all this was happening, the noise was registering in the telephone and was not lost on the operator.

"What is happening?" she asked.

I reported that the machine had just given up all its earnings for the past few months, at least.

"Sir," she said " will you please put the coins back in the box."

"Operator," I said, "if you give me your name and address I will be glad to mail you the coins."

The veterans exploded with cheers.

One of the doctors stood up. "Tell me," he said, "when you came in this room a half hour or so ago, how many of you were experiencing your normal chronic pains?" More than half the veterans in the room raised their hands.

"Now," said the doctor, "how many of you, in the past five or ten minutes, discovered that these chronic pains receded or disappeared?"

The same hands, it appeared to me, went up again.

Why should simple laughter have produced this effect? Brain researchers speculate that laughter activates release of endorphins, the body's own pain-reducing chemicals that are very similar to morphine. The veterans were experiencing the same positive effects I had in my own illness years earlier.

Subsequent medical studies throughout the world verify what Norman Cousins has written. No one is suggesting that laughter paves the way for immortality, only that it makes the stay here more enjoyable.

Again, what about the workplace? If humor improves personal well being, improves physical and mental health, and reduces health care costs, it bodes well for people, even those who employ people. (Reducing turnover and burnout can only help employers.)

When these findings are validated by solid statistical evidence from the medical community, work organizations will immediately try to integrate humor into "wellness" programs. If this means that the effort will be limited to issuing joke books to employees, organizations will once again miss the concepts of connectedness and perspective.

Chapter Three

Your Job

The word "job" is named after a Biblical character who had considerable woes. Although this is a stretch of history, no one would dispute that a good deal of patience is required for work survival.

With that established then why do we work at a job?

To alleviate your fears that this reasonably priced publication has no intellectual base I now turn to the famous hierarchy of needs developed by Abraham Maslow.

Here is how this theory actually operates in the workplace:

On the bottom rung there is good old basic physiological needs: Groceries, shelter, and sex. At the work place you make money so you can buy groceries and beverages. The longer hours you work at a place, the more shelter you will have during that period. There are also other benefits. You can save money by using company rest rooms, toilet paper, and towels. Most places also have free drinking water and first aid kits with Band-Aids.

The next rung in the hierarchy is security. Very simply these are the people that check your passes and look for breaches. Often they have the ability to stare at television monitors expressionlessly. (This look is worth pursuing if you are interested in that career path.) Do nothing to wake up the security people. There is another meaning of security in organizations, rendered archaic by the new techniques of downsizing, restructuring, and reengineering.

The third rung is social. Massive potlucks and holiday parties prevail. Do not expect to see the same groups of people at these various get-togethers.

Esteem needs are the fourth rung. Greed and envy come with the promotions of others. Those people promoted no longer lunch with the troops. Here are some of the signs: recognition through bonuses, vacations at exotic places, swimming pools, power moves, and partying with beautiful people. There are some people who have internal self esteem who feel good about themselves no matter what the boss does or says. They are under study.

Self-actualization. Win-win. Both you and the organization succeed. You are doing exactly what you always wanted to do since you were twelve years old. Somewhere between 13 and 14 percent of us get this experience on the job. If we have one of these jobs we are actually glad when our peers are promoted as long as they let us stay in place being a mechanic, a number cruncher, a computer hack, or whatever we think is the greatest. (This person would do these things all weekend too if the significant other or the little people at home would let her/him.)

Note the shortened pictorial version of the hierarchy of needs in Figure 2, which is inverted for no special reason.

Revised Hierarchy of Needs for the Workplace
(with apologies to Maslow)

Basic Needs: Food, Coffee, Sex...
(Caution: food and coffee not permitted near computers)

401K
(A security plan that allows ex-employees to eat
until finding other employment)

Potlucks, Cocktails
and Health Bars
(Meeting social needs in the company)

Perks
(Employee of the month parking
and other items of envy)

.

(Self actualization
with a PC)

Why Do You Work?

With this theory as backdrop look at the practical ramifications. Seriously now, why do people really work? More importantly, why do you work?

If you had the time you would most likely respond with the following suggestions:

"I LIKE THE LARGER CREAMIER DOUBLE FLAVOR OREOS RATHER THAN THE SINGLE, CHEAPER VARIETY."

"SO THE CLERKS AT NORDSTROMS WILL CONTINUE TO KNOW ME BY MY FIRST NAME. THEY MIGHT ALSO GO BROKE IF I DON'T SHOP THERE."

"SO THE GOVERNMENT WON'T HAVE TO OVERTAX THE WEALTHY."

"I USED TO WORK BECAUSE I DIDN'T WANT TO BE TRAPPED AT HOME WITH MY KIDS, BUT NOW I'M SO USED TO WORKING I WORK THREE JOBS."

"TO PAY CHILDCARE SO I CAN WORK IN ORDER TO PAY CHILDCARE SO I CAN WORK…"

"TO HAVE THE MONEY TO SUPPORT MY HOBBIES AND ALL THE THINGS I ENJOY IN LIFE."

"BECAUSE IF MY WIFE EVER FOUND I HAD ANY TIME OFF SHE WOULD 'HONEY DO' ME TO DEATH."

"SO I CAN TALK LIKE AN ADULT."

"SO MY BOSS CAN MAKE MORE MONEY."

"SO I CAN BECOME EMPLOYEE OF THE MONTH AND HAVE MY OWN PARKING PLACE."

"IT IS A WONDERFUL PLACE TO SHOW OFF BABIES."

"SO I CAN ESTABLISH CREDIT."

"A GREAT PLACE TO BARTER, BORROW, AND LEARN ABOUT THINGS TO BUY."

"SO I CAN KNOW MORE ABOUT ERGONOMICS."

"SO THAT I HAVE A REASON TO GO TO HAPPY HOUR."

"TO MAKE COPIES OF RECIPES."

"SO THAT I CAN HAVE A LIFE STYLE."

"SO I CAN HAVE A PAGER."

"SO THE GRANDCHILDREN WILL HAVE A LITTLE SOMETHING UNDER THE CHRISTMAS TREE, A LITTLE SOMETHING OF EVERYTHING."

"SO I DON'T HAVE TO COOK EVERY NIGHT."

"TO KEEP MY HUSBAND FROM YELLING AT ME FOR SPENDING MONEY WE DON'T HAVE."

"I LIKE TO BUY CD'S AND LOTS OF STUFF FOR MY COMPUTER, BUT I WORK SO MUCH THAT I DON'T HAVE TIME TO LISTEN OR USE THEM, BUT THEY LOOK GOOD IN MY HOUSE."

"SO MY KID AND I CAN BOTH GO NUTS WITH COMPUTER GAMES."

"TO MAKE SURE MY BOSS HAS SOMETHING TO KEEP HIM OCCUPIED."

"SO I HAVE AN EXCUSE FOR WHY MY HOUSE ISN'T CLEAN."

"I LIKE THE COMMUTE."

"I LOVE CAFETERIA FOOD."

" I OWE I OWE...OFF TO WORK I GO."

"TO GO TO THE BEACH SO I CAN COLLECT SHELLS."

"KID'S MUSIC LESSONS."

"TO WORK WITH UPPER MANAGEMENT."

"BECAUSE MY STUFF WON'T FIT IN A GROCERY SHOPPING CART."

"SO I CAN AFFORD A RADAR DETECTOR, A CELLULAR PHONE, AND AT LEAST ONE LATTE EVERY DAY."

"TO PAY FOR ADDITIONAL CABLE CHANNELS."

"HABIT."

"TO KEEP ROLAIDS IN BUSINESS."

"MY WANTS OVERPOWER MY NEEDS."

"GIVES ME A BREAK FROM MY TIME OFF."

"GIVES ME A PLACE TO LEAVE AT LUNCH."

"HELP BALANCE THE DEFICIT—THEIRS AND MINE."

"SO I CAN PAY THE SPEEDING TICKET I GOT WHILE DRIVING HOME FROM WORK."

"SO I CAN RETIRE AT SEVENTY-FIVE AND REALLY LIVE."

"THE KNEEHOLE IN MY DESK PROVIDES A SAFE HAVEN FROM STRESS."

"SO I CAN HEAR ABOUT QUALITY, EXCELLENCE, WORLD CLASS, LEARNING ORGANIZATIONS, AND EMPOWERMENT AND DREAM ABOUT IT AT NIGHTS."

"THE MEETINGS THERE PROVIDE ME THE OPPORTUNITY TO MAKE SHOPPING LISTS."

"TO LET MY BOSS PRACTICE HER SUPERVISORY SKILLS."

"TO SUPPORT MY DELI."

"TO SEE IF THIS IS THE DAY I WILL MEET NEW AND INTERESTING PEOPLE."

"TO SPREAD MY TALENT AROUND."

"FOR THE EXOTIC BLEND COFFEE AT BREAKS."

"TO CATCH UP ON GOSSIP ABOUT PEOPLE I JUST MET."

"TO HAVE MY HAIR DONE."

"I DON'T REMEMBER."

"TO GIVE US ACCESS TO TUITION AID PROGRAMS SO THAT WE CAN TAKE COURSES LIKE STRESS MANAGEMENT."

"WHEN I WAS LITTLE MY PARENTS TOLD ME I HAD TO."

"TO ATTEND THE OFFICE HOLIDAY PARTY AND WONDER IF THE DISCUSSION ABOUT SEXUAL HARASSMENT IS ONLY A PASSING PHASE."

"IT GIVES ME SOMETHING TO COMPLAIN ABOUT TO MY SIGNIFICANT OTHER."

"WORK GIVES ME A PLACE TO COMPLAIN ABOUT MY SIGNIFICANT OTHER."

So there you have it. There are experts lecturing that people work for achievement, recognition, and responsibility. This could be, but real people, such as those quoted above, have a wider perspective.

Your Job in Perspective

It is extremely important in the scheme of things to have a job and give it importance. The worst thing that can happen to you is to say, "I don't have a job." You can be between engagements, but don't say unemployed. Although the response "I work in the home" may get you off the hook for a while, it is suspect. Notice how people subjected to "early retirement" schemes come up with "research" or "consulting" in addressing the question.

You believe this to be an overstatement? The job really isn't that important? What is the first thing you are asked when you meet someone? Yes. "What do you do?" Not, what music do you like? Not, what are your favorite sports? Not, tell me about your family? Those kinds of questions only come later when we decide if it's important to discuss this with you, after, of course, determining if what you "do" is important.

Give it some thought. It really is not very important what you do but what you say you do. Salesperson is wrong. Account executive is still in. Everyone is professional. No one is amateur. You should see yourself as an expediter/associate rather than a clerk. You're not a word processor but an analyst—maybe even a systems analyst. If you live in a cubical at work indicate your office is the latest in open management.

At social get togethers you'll be surprised how many people will talk to you if you have a long and mysterious title.

You get the picture. Take all these things seriously but don't forget to laugh about them too, because your job is serious but you don't have to be.

It is entirely possible that your job isn't serious either.

However, humor consultants tell you to take your job seriously. (Businesses wouldn't hire them if they said something else.)

To put everything in perspective, however, think of all the horrible things that could happen to you at work. Then add: "So then what."

Here are some to work with:

- IRATE CUSTOMER SWEARS AND THREATENS TO THROW MERCHANDISE AT YOU. (IF YOU KNOW HOW TO FORCE YOUR BODY TO EXECUTE ON COMMAND, THIS WOULD BE THE TIME TO VOMIT.)

- BE PUT ON PROBATION. (ALTHOUGH IT'S SIMILAR TO HOUSE ARREST, YOU CAN GO HOME IN THE EVENINGS.)

- BEING PASSED OVER FOR PROMOTION. (YOU GET TO KEEP YOUR JOB WHEN THE PROMOTED LAYER OF MANAGEMENT IS FIRED.)

- SPEND THE REST OF MY LIFE WORKING WHERE I AM. (IMPOSSIBLE. THE ODDS ARE YOUR ORGANIZATION ISN'T GOING TO BE AROUND THAT LONG.)

- WALK OUT OF THE REST ROOM WITH MY SKIRT TUCKED IN MY PANTY HOSE. (MAYBE YOU WOULD GET MORE DATES OR GET A JOB DANCING.)

- HARD DRIVE CRASHES AND I HAVEN'T BACKED UP FOR A MONTH. (THIS GIVES YOU ANOTHER MONTH'S EMPLOYMENT RE-CONSTRUCTING.)

- PEOPLE COULD STOP BUYING OUR PRODUCT. (WE COULD GET HUGE HAMMERS, SMASH THE PRODUCTS, AND SELL THEM TO SINGAPORE FOR JUNK.)

- BE SUSPENDED WITH OR WITHOUT PAY. (YOU HOPE THEY WILL LET YOU DOWN WHEN YOU HAVE TO GO TO THE REST ROOM.)

- BEING NAMED A PRINCIPAL IN AN OFFICE SCANDAL. (CALL HOME. IT'S BETTER THAN BEING THERE.)

- IN YOUR JOB AS A PAINTER YOU PAINTED THE HOUSE THE WRONG COLOR. (EVERYONE KNOWS THAT THE FINAL COLOR NEVER MATCHES THE CHIP.)

- YOU COULD GET FIRED. (YOU ALWAYS WANTED TO LIVE IN A COMMUNE.)

- YOUR BOSS CUTS YOUR EXPENSES FOR TRAVEL. (YOU MIGHT MAKE IT UP BY SELLING THE COMPANY PENS YOU HAVE ACCUMULATED AT HOME.)

- DIE AND WAKE UP AND FIND HELL IS WHERE YOU WORK. (BEFORE IT IS TOO LATE YOU MIGHT CONSIDER CHANGING JOBS.)

Handling Exit Interviews

Let's imagine for a moment that you lost your job because of layoffs, re-structuring, the boss's spouse, or you were just fired.

Your organization may have exit interviews. (You can check this out in something called a HR handbook. HR means Human Reductions.) If they do, you can restore your self-esteem easily.

Try these as vehicles for leaving the organization:

- "I'M GLAD IT HAPPENED. NOW I CAN CONCENTRATE ON SELLING MY POETRY."

- "IT WAS BOUND TO HAPPEN. TOO MANY PEOPLE WERE ENVIOUS."

- "THE HOURS OF WORK DIDN'T WORK OUT WITH MY BOYFRIEND."

- "I'VE MADE A GOAL OF STAYING ONLY TWENTY-FOUR MONTHS WITH ANY GROUP."

- "THE OFFICE WAS STUFFY AND THE VIEW WAS NOT GOOD."

- "No eligible men."

- "My live-in moved out so my expenses went down."

- "Thought I would like to work in the mainstream."

- "The Midwest has always appealed to me."

- "Every hour was rush hour."

- "I want to work someplace where I don't make so much money."

- "I'm going to win the lottery this summer."

- "My supervisor expected me to work, even when it was inconvenient for me."

- "I didn't want to stay here so long that it would be possible for me to file an age discrimination suit."

- "I didn't have time to make entries in my diary."

- "I got a rash every time I got within ten feet of another employee. This employee was my supervisor."

- "Now I can go on stage."

Dealing With Employment People

So now we face a dilemma. Someone always wants to know why you resigned, quit, were fired, or reengineered. This someone could be just a close friend or someone who is counting on you to pay for groceries. This is explainable. You will require more skill in dealing with employment people in HR organizations, who would like to find reasons for not hiring you. That's their job.

In anticipation of this happening it is important for you to have answers for their questions. Of course irreverence is not appropriate, but you can look for ways to bring perspective to the table.

So now to their questions:

Why did you leave your last job? Try something like: "Well, sir, it left me." Try to be woeful but not tearful; too much emotion can bring compassion but no job offer. Here is another possible answer: "I drove up to the building where I worked and found it had been moved during the night and there was no forwarding address." (Be careful with this one. They will check.)

"What suggestions did you leave your old boss where you worked?" This is an effort to get you to say something negative about your old boss. A good direct answer like "Oh she was young and very attractive" may buy you a little time. A close out answer would be: "I promised to look for a job for her as well."

"What achievements were you proud of?" Watch this one. They may not think that your answer—you managed to avoid burn-out—is a significant achievement. Tell them that you had the highest rate of return of anyone on the production line. (Those kind of words normally appeal to business people; hopefully, they will not understand what you just said.)

"Who was the best boss you ever had?" Answering your "first spouse" is probably inappropriate. Obviously the next question is going to be "Why?" Figure out an answer ahead of time such as: "My first boss was super because he left me alone. He had his own moonlight business and was too tired during the day."

"Who was your worst boss?" This is where you might find out if the interviewer indeed has a sense of humor. Try "older sister." You may get signals that this is not appropriate, particularly if the interviewer was an older sister. So be ready to say: "I was only kidding. My worst boss was a person who gave me very close supervision all the time because he had my job before he got promoted."

"What ups and downs have you had the last few years?" This is a clever way of asking you whether you've been out ill much. A factual

answer is okay here. "My temperature has ranged between 98.2 and 102.2 degrees."

"What are your greatest strengths and weaknesses?" They want to construct your psychological profile. Be straightforward. "I can bench-press one hundred pounds and do very well on parallel bars. My knees are weak and bother me when I try to touch my toes." (The fact that you are trying to touch your toes may or may not be an asset. Gauge this response on your assessment of whether the interviewer can touch her/his toes.)

"Why so many job changes?" They believe you are unstable. Try this. "My jobs were all exported overseas. I am hoping that those that went to emerging countries will come back."

"Why aren't you making more money with your qualifications?" In today's economy this isn't a fair question. However, here is a possibility for you: "Even though I have a master's degree in drama I've never been able to act as well as bosses would like. I know that your organization would provide a perfect stage for the unique abilities, interests, and qualifications that I bring with me. And of course, you know, money isn't everything."

"Where do you want to be in five years?" They want to know about your ambition. Supposedly they hire for the opening they have, but some interviewers are more aggressive. Go for it. "Yes, I'd like to be president. If I get there I want you to know that I like you very much and I will take you with me."

"Why should we want to hire you?" Here is your no-nonsense answer: "I am personable, intelligent, and work hard." You might add: "I am also very humble. I know my previous statement didn't sound that way, but I know you want me to tell it like it is."

No matter how well you do in an interview, they may not hire you.

Here are some habits or activities to avoid:

- WRITING YOUR RESUME WITH A SCENTED MARKER.

- EXCESSIVE SOBBING.

- WEARING AN ORANGE AND BLACK CHECKERED SUIT, EVEN IF IT IS THE SCHOOL COLORS OF THE HR INTERVIEWER.

- SAYING SWELL, RIGHT-ON, COOL, OUTRAGEOUS, OR RAD.

- SAYING, "GOSH THAT WAS A GOOD QUESTION" AND RECORDING IT ON YOUR LAPTOP COMPUTER.

- COLORING YOUR HAIR PURPLE.

- PEDDLING YOUR BASEBALL CARDS.

- INVITING THE INTERVIEWER TO YOUR CHURCH.

- RHYMING YOUR RESUME.

- RECORDING YOUR INTERVIEW.

- TAKING A CALL FROM ANOTHER EMPLOYER ON YOUR CELLULAR PHONE.

- WEARING A SKI MASK.

So much for your job. Getting one. Keeping one. Losing one. And looking for another. Even here, there is humor in the process.

Success in the Workplace

There is nothing wrong with being successful at work. What is uproariously funny, however, is what some will do for upward mobility. Career pathing via company politics is an art form.

How to Succeed in Business Without Really Trying, the classic business humor novel (later a musical) by Shepherd Mead, features Pierrepont Finch, an "all around" man of no special ability who rises to the top. Early in his career he remembers to use the elevator to his advantage when talking to a top boss:

"DAMNED FINE MEMO OF YOURS ON THE WICKET SITUATION, SIR," HE SAYS.

"OH, YOU LIKE IT UM...ER..

"FINCH, SIR. PIERREPONT FINCH. I AGREED WITH ALMOST ALL OF YOUR RECOMMENDATIONS..."

Later on Finch reveals a few more secrets:

PICK THE RIGHT TEAM. LOYALTY IS GOOD AS LONG AS YOUR PERSON MOVES UP FAST ENOUGH TO LEAVE PLENTY OF ROOM BEHIND.

MEMORIZE SIMPLE PHRASES WHEN DEALING WITH STATISTICS: "THERE'S EVERY REASON TO BELIEVE THAT THE 'DON'T CARES' ARE WITH US."

STAB THE RIGHT BACKS. GUARD YOUR OWN BACK.

CHOOSE YOUR SPOUSE CAREFULLY. IF FORCED TO REPLACE, DO IT BETWEEN JOBS.

GET THE SAME HOBBY AS YOUR TOP BOSS.

Pierrepont introduces the latter idea this way:

"GOT TO HURRY HOME, SIR. THE LITTLE DEVILS ARE WHELPING."

"WHELPING, FINCH? DON'T TELL ME YOU'RE A MONGOOSE MAN!"

"ARE YOU TOO, SIR? WE ARE A RARE BREED AREN'T WE? TELL ME, DO YOU FAVOR SNAKE MEAT OR KIPPERS?"

Finch does not have all the answers. *Here is an expansion of rules for your success:*

Enthusiastically embrace every new program coming out of headquarters. If TCC (Total Capitulation to Customers) is the new melody, you lead the orchestra. Here is a cautionary note: Be willing and able to change in a nanosecond (and quickly too). If the tune changes to SAB (Shareowners Are Beautiful), get out the marching music.

Play the company sport. (Caution: Even if bowling is acceptable, it is never appropriate for upward mobility.)

Network with executive secretaries. In exchange for information they supply about top executives, feed them gossip about your peers.

You can cultivate friends in higher places to replace those you lose. Since there are fewer people in higher places, you have fewer friends. Since friends often get in your way, this is desirable.

De-rail your subordinates, particularly those who appear to have potential. Transfer them to Glendive, Montana, for "field experience." Leave them there.

Walk by all the bosses offices on weekends, at least until you establish who comes in. It is not necessary for you to do any work on weekends, just be seen. An all purpose statement when seen by a boss could be: "Sorry to bother you, sir, but do you have any last minute ideas for us before we embark on the fantastic new _____ (fill in blank with marketing, expense reduction, restructuring, empowerment, etc.) program you've come up with ?" (If one of the bosses is a woman, don't say sir.)

Success is often tabulated by numbers of sales, production targets met, due dates met, and other such useful tools. If there is any humor there it lies, not with the numbers, but in what people do with the measurement systems. We have all heard of the salespersons who have gone all out to sell huge quantities of items to win sales trips to exotic places. One I'm familiar with sold a three-year supply of toilet paper to a grocery chain. He won the sales prize and, because of a huge inventory, the chain had a special every week on toilet paper.

Imagine a run on toilet paper.

Every week.

You can be successful and ethical at the same time. After a long meeting on the importance of honesty in achieving results, one middle manager said, "I'm all for ethics if it improves results."

So there you have it. You, your job, and your twist to it are incredibly important, particularly when you cultivate a sense of humor. It is still possible that you need additional help. With this in mind I have put together twenty-six ways to cope with stress. Why twenty-six ways? When you add your own list of twenty-six you will be playing with a full deck.

Twenty-six ways to Cope With Stress

1. CLEAN YOUR EARS OUT WITH YOUR GLOVE COMPARTMENT CAR KEY.

2. OFFER A BLACKHEAD INSPECTION SERVICE IN YOUR HUMAN RESOURCES OFFICE SO YOU CAN HAVE A BLACKHEAD-FREE WORK ENVIRONMENT.

3. STAMP "SAVE" ON EVERY SHEET OF TOILET TISSUE IN THE OFFICE REST ROOMS, SUPPORTING THE NEED TO SAVE ON EXPENSES.

4. STAPLE THREE MEMOS TOGETHER ON UNRELATED SUBJECTS WITH THE DIRECTIVE: "CORRELATE AND EXPEDITE."

5. SINCE WORK RELATED SUBJECTS KEEP YOU AWAKE AT NIGHT, FEEL FREE TO NAP AT THE OFFICE.

6. TELL YOUR BOSS THAT YOU WILL NOT BE IN TODAY BECAUSE YOU OFTEN GET SICK ON FRIDAYS.

7. SEND A GET WELL CARD FROM THE OFFICE STAFF WHENEVER THE BOSS EXPLODES.

8. CLICK OR GRIND YOUR TEETH TO THE MELODY OF THE WILLIAM TELL OVERTURE.

9. PERIODICALLY CRUMPLE UP CIGARETTE PACKS AND LEAVE CIGARETTE BUTTS IN LOCATIONS WHERE NO SMOKING IS ALLOWED.

10. SHAVE ONLY HALF OF YOUR FACE AND TELL THOSE AROUND YOU THAT YOU HAVE A BETTER HALF.

11. PUT MAKE-UP ON HALF OF YOUR FACE AND TELL PEOPLE YOU ARE GOING TO BE TWO-FACED TODAY.

12. GET A HAIR CUT ON COMPANY TIME (SINCE IT GROWS ON COMPANY TIME).

13. REPEAT OVER AND OVER AGAIN: MICE BLIND THREE, RUN THEY HOW SEE.

14. DRIVE A NEW WAY TO WORK THROUGH HONOLULU.

15. SEND THE POWER COMPANY BILL TO THE GAS COMPANY, THE GAS COMPANY BILL TO VISA, THE PHONE COMPANY BILL TO THE CABLE COMPANY, ETC. (EACH ENCLOSED WITH A CHECK FOR $1.95.)

16. INITIATE A PETITION DRIVE DEMANDING THAT WALKING SHOES BE DESIGNATED THE STATE SHOE FOR ALL WORKERS.

17. WHEN YOUR BOSS SWEARS ADVISE HIM THAT YOU DON'T CARE BUT THAT IT IS A VIOLATION OF THE CLEAN AIR ACT.

18. PUT YOUR GLASSES ON YOUR FOREHEAD AND INSIST THAT SOMEONE HAS TAKEN YOUR GLASSES.

19. BRING IN A FIRE HOSE TO CLEAN UP THE LUNCH ROOM.

20. TELL THE PERSON YOU'RE TALKING TO ON THE PHONE THAT YOU HAVE A CALL-WAITING CALL YOU HAVE TO TAKE SO HE/SHE CAN EITHER HANG UP OR CALL YOU BACK AT WHICH TIME SHE/HE WILL BE A CALL-WAITING CALLER AND THEN YOU CAN TAKE THEIR CALL.

21. PUT A NEW SPIN ON THE MYSTERY OF HIS PROMOTION.

22. RUB YOURSELF WITH LOW FAT MARGARINE AND TELL PEOPLE YOU'RE SPREADING YOURSELF THIN.

23. WEAR SUSPENDERS OVER YOUR SHOULDERS BUT DO NOT ATTACH THEM TO YOUR PANTS OR SLACKS. (PEERS WILL MARVEL AT THE SUSPENSE OF IT ALL.)

24. WALK AROUND WITH A MOUTH FULL OF SMOKE; WHEN APPROPRIATE BLOW SMOKE RINGS, AND YELL FIRE.

25. GET EARRINGS THAT WILL HOLD QUARTERS FOR PARKING METERS.

26. WHEN SOMEONE SAYS "HAVE A NICE DAY," TELL THEM THAT ISN'T WHAT YOU HAD IN MIND.

Chapter Four

Organizations: Off The Wall

Organizations are funny. Absolutely.

As far back as we can establish, most of them were started by human beings. This is true even of agencies created by federal and state governments. Bureaucracies just do not happen. They need people who create humor without realizing it. They then become organizations that also create humor without realizing it.

There are people out there, however, who realize what they are doing, encouraging and stimulating humor at every opportunity.

Sam Walton, the late president of Wal Mart said:

"Celebrate your successes. Find some humor in your failures. Don't take yourself so seriously. Loosen up and everybody around you will loosen up. Have fun. Show enthusiasm always. When all else fails, put on a costume and sing a silly song. Then make everyone sing with you. Don't do a hula on Wall Street. It's been done. Think up your own stunt. All of this is more important, and more fun than you think, and it really fools the competition. 'Why should we take those cornballs at Wal Mart seriously.'" (In a challenge to his employees, Walton offered, if they made or exceeded earnings projections, to dance a hula on Wall Street. They did and he did.)

Tom Melohn at North American Tool and Die says: "We set three objectives for NATD. First, we planned to grow the company profitably. Second to share the wealth among employees. And third, and equally critical, it was important to have fun—not just the two owners, but all our employees. And that is the key. To have fun."

Bill Gore, the late CEO of W. L. Gore and Associates said: "The objective of our enterprise is universally agreed upon: to earn money and have fun doing it. The two are intimately tied together."

Tom Monaghan, founder of Domino's Pizza, reaffirms this. One day he told Tom Peters that he had added a ninth point to Peter's and Waterman's eight ways to build an excellent company: "Have fun."

Management consultant and author Tom Peters say this in his book, *Thriving on Chaos:*

"One form of emotional involvement, laughter, deserves a special comment. Urgency and laughter go hand in glove.... To speed action taking, we simply must learn to laugh at our own (personal, organizational) bureaucratic, action delaying foibles, and we must learn to laugh at interesting and useful mistakes.... In general, a spirited environment is marked by laughter—enthusiasm for being on a team and trying darn near anything to make the service or product better."

Southwest Airlines and its leader Herb Kelleher provide us an inspirational story of organizational success. Note the role of humor in this piece by *Fortune* magazine writer Kenneth Labich:

"Southwest workers often go out of their way to amuse, surprise, or somehow entertain passengers. During delays at the gate, ticket agents will award prizes to the passenger with the largest hole in his or her sock. Flight attendants have been known to hide in the overhead luggage bins and then pop out when passengers start filing onboard.

Veteran Southwest fliers looking for a few yuks have learned to listen up to announcements over the intercom. A recent effort:

"Good morning, ladies and gentlemen. Those of you who wish to smoke will please file out to our lounge on the wing, where you can enjoy our feature film, *Gone With The Wind*."

On the same flight, an attendant later made this announcement:

"Please pass all plastic cups to the center aisle so we can wash them out and use them for the next group of passengers."

For every Southwest Airlines there are five hundred companies with no corporate sense of humor. Said another way, people who work for these organizations are—with our apologies to *Fortune*—the unfortunate 500.

Many large businesses grew from one person with an idea. "Watson, come here" created, among other things, a telephone bureaucracy with nearly one million people, most of whom had a sense of humor at least until the 1984 divestiture resulting in new corporate lineups. Market analysts called the new AT&T and the Seven Bell Companies Snow White and the Seven Dwarfs. Telephone company insiders renamed the companies: **Taco Bell**, (Southwest), **Southern Belle**, (Southern Bell) **Cow Bell**, (Midwest), **Liberty Bell**, (Mid-Atlantic), **Yankee Bell**, (New England, New York), **Wild Bell**, (Northwestern, Mountain, Pacific Northwest), and **Tinker Bell** (Pacific Telephone in California).

How To Organize

Here are some additional ways to organize:

1. Geography. Your group reports to someone who reports to someone who is headquartered in Livermore. There is the western division (sometimes referred to as the California and other groups), the mountain division, the Mid-west river division, the Far East division, and perhaps a Southern division. Now nothing is very funny about that until you try to communicate with one another. The language, the dialect, the slang, and the "pushiness" of those "other" people are "so transparent." Why? Because the axis of the business runs through your division. Properly so. Right? The rationale for this organization is to "bring people closer to customers."

2. Product. The headquarters for each product line can be anywhere. Each product is unique and sold to potential customers, perhaps the same customers as other products in the business (by salespeople in other divisions). The rationale here is "to bring customers closer to your product."

3. Function. This organization could have a manufacturing or service function, an engineering function, or an accounting and sales function. It might also have staff functions such as (normally in capital letters) Human Resources, Public Relations, Legal, and/or Security. It could even have a World Class Quality function. The basis for this kind of organization is "to bring departments closer to departments."

The explanations for any reorganizations include (1) "hands on" management ("We just had a complaint from a customer in Mt. Vernon"), (2) a need to consolidate ("We need to be closer to the financial district in Albany"), and (3) develop new product lines ("We need to be closer to the emerging market in Prague").

It is inappropriate to suggest that there is not a lot of imagination in organization structure. Suppose, however, that businesses and government organized by:

Eye Color? Would people see eye to eye better? Would our organization be able to see gray and green as well as black and white?

Hair? Clairol would permit transfer from one group to another. Discrimination against bald people would be prohibited. (They could, however, be apportioned so no one group would be penalized because they had too many.)

Height? The preferred groups would be 5' to 5'4", 5'5" to 5'10", 5'11" to 6'5", and over 6'6". People could reach new heights within each group.

Age? (Old boy, girl network; boomers; have nots; the busts; generation x) Some parts of the organization would have to change. For example, senior employees, and products or services with lower shelf lives would be matched.

Gender? Could certainly save on the number of specialized rest rooms.

Birth Order? Department heads and the CEO will be first-born children. (They learned to direct and control at an early age.) Middle children will mediate. Younger children might survive in a public relations or advertising niche.

Alphabetical? A to F, G to M, N to Z. No discrimination of people, products, or service would exist here. This would necessitate some reassignment because of the oversupply of Smiths, Jones, and Petersons.

Glasses, No Glasses, Contacts? This would have a long-term impact on noses and whether or not they became larger or broader. Corporate visions would have a place here. So would what we know about super vision.

There are a number of ways of organizing, equally as efficient—all conducive to humor. Admittedly, it is not easy to understand the concepts or building blocks of organizations, bureaucracy, or entrepreneurship. Some say it is too much of a stretch of credibility to say that organizations are the hotbed of humor.

We will go on record. They are.

Off the Wall

Most organizations have an element of being "off the wall." You readily recognize this since you are now an accomplished practitioner of humor. In figure 5 we have put two lists together, words that may help you describe your organization. There is usually a tie-in of the two lists. The third list also comes from your organization but it is often incongruous (off the wall) with the first two lists.

Your task here is to come up with "off the wall" suggestions for the third list. Here is an example: Wall I is Production, Wall II is The Boss is Coming, and Wall III could be: The trouble left here okay. Give it a try.

Figure 5

Walls

Wall I	*Wall II*	*Off the Wall*
Production	The Boss is Coming	_____
In Basket	Bulletin Board	_____
Health	No Smoking	_____
Fax	Copy	_____
Communicate	Two way	_____
Inspire	Motivate	_____
Boss	Supervisor	_____

Computer	Yes/No	_____
See No Evil	Hear No Evil	_____
Lie	Cover	_____
Elastic	Belt	_____
Constant	Steady	_____
Auditors	IRS	_____
Memos	Bureaucratic	_____
Constant Improvement	Standardization	_____
Shallow	Lack of Depth	_____
Management by Objective	Management by Excellence	_____
Whole Nine Yards	Expand	_____
Work Hard	Play Hard	_____
Conference	Meeting	_____
Briefs	Skirt Suits	_____
Collar/tie	Choke	_____
Foxes	Fixes	_____
Tires	Cement	_____
Inter-regional	Inter-company	_____

"Off the wall" may be too cavalier for some. Figure 6 offers another approach: List one, List two, and Listless.

Figure 6:

Checkout List

List I	List II	Listless
Pitch	Strike	_____
Brokers	Editors	_____
Authoritarian	Dictator	_____
Communication	Restricted	_____
Straining	Training	_____
Promotion	Sales Contest	_____
Boating	Ocean	_____
Intellectual	Pedantic	_____
Analytical	Rational	_____
Organization	Structure	_____
Crest	Wave	_____
Shiftless	Lazy	_____
Perspective	Supervision	_____
Inventory	Cost Containment	_____
Labor	Relations	_____
Hackles	Temper	_____
Office	Plant	_____
Ponderous	Commuting	_____

You can find potential "off the wall" and "listless" responses in Appendix B. One sequence, Management by Objective, Management by Excellence, and MBBS—Management by Best Seller is a favorite.

What's In

Lest we irritate some management gurus, we think Mssrs. Maslow, Hertzberg, McGregor, Likert, McClelland, Drucker, Peters, Deming, Senge and others have contributed mightily to management knowledge and understanding. Their wisdom should be listened to and, where appropriate, applied.

What is funny, however, is that many organizations seem to be content with lesser lights. They take the current "packages" as the end all solution for all management problems.

Here's how it works. Whether it's MBO, Management Development, Excellence, Total Quality Management, Statistical Analysis, Team Building, Just in Time, Japanese Management, or Continuous Improvement, organizations will go all out to implement whatever is hot to the absolute exclusion of whatever happened before—even ten minutes before. All the binders from previous training program are removed.

One of the great improvements and cost savings, however, is that organizations no longer throw out the old binders. They discard the old material but they reuse the binders for the new program. Discovered by accident by a clerk, the concept has spread like home pages on the internet. The new binder business is no longer lucrative.

We suggest that employees are skeptical about these changes and wonder if management is losing it. So they laugh. Although no one has high expectations, it is still possible that some organizations may resolve to retain the best of all the management seers.

Management by objective, hula hoops, intra-preneurship, color tests of personality, theory x, y, and z, pet rocks, benevolent management, employment by silhouette (women) and 46 long (men), human relations, and leisure suits are probably out.

In further speculation, do you think synergy, strategic planning, mainframe, quantity, engineers, skunkworks, empowerment, and back to basics are still in? Certainly corporate culture, total quality management, visions, demassing, global competition, team building, and restructuring will be with us for a year or two.

It's just possible the concept of being a person, open, accessible, and smiling will come back. Perhaps some of these values will come back with new words.

This leads us to the next millennium. Please advise those around you that you heard it here first. Sometime in the Twenty-first Century these important concepts will be introduced by the phrase Management By:

- TOP LEVEL MANAGERS WILL BE BENCH MARKING, LOOKING FOR NEW IDEAS IN OTHER LOCATIONS, I.E. SUN VALLEY, THE SWISS ALPS, THE FJORDS OF NORWAY, AND GREECE. AS A RESULT, DECISIONS WILL BE MADE RANDOMLY BY SOMEONE IN THE OFFICE. IT WILL BE CALLED MANAGEMENT BY ABANDONMENT. **(MBA)**

- ALL DECISIONS WILL BE MADE BY COMPUTER. BY THE YEAR 2050 THE THINKING COMPUTER WILL BE AS SMART AND LITERATE AS THE AVERAGE FOURTH GRADER. MANAGEMENT BY ARTIFICIAL INTELLIGENCE **(MBAI)** WILL PREVAIL. THIS WILL EVENTUALLY GIVE GROUND TO MANAGEMENT BY OFF-LINE. **(MBOL)**

- BUILDING ON COMPETITION, THE TOUGH GET GOING, SURVIVAL OF THE FITTEST, GLOBAL COMPETITION, AND DOG-EAT-DOG, A NEW MANAGERIAL PHILOSOPHY WILL EMERGE. IT WILL BE CALLED MANAGEMENT BY FOOD CHAIN. **(MBFC).** ANOTHER THEORIST WILL WRITE A BOOK CALLED MANAGEMENT BY NATURAL SELECTION. **(MBNS)**

- THE AUTHOR OF ANOTHER MANAGEMENT THEORY IS NOW IN GRADUATE SCHOOL AT A LEADING UNIVERSITY. AS A MATTER OF FACT, SHE IS WRITING HER THESIS ON THE VALUE OF SECOND GUESSING ALL MANAGEMENT DECISIONS. THE TITLE WILL BE MANAGEMENT BY POST MORTEM SEMINAR. **(MBPMS)**

- UTILIZING POLLS, MAN ON THE STREET/WOMAN ON THE STREET INTERVIEWS, TALK SHOWS, AND CHAT GROUPS ON THE INTERNET, A REMARKABLE MANAGEMENT THEORY WILL EVOLVE. LOOK FOR MANAGEMENT BY BLUE SKY. (MBBS)

Thanks to discoveries like these in the past, twentieth century management has made some progress. After all, in the nineteenth century people were "hands" and supervisors were "overseers." Then we progressed to the scientific management school where people, like raw materials, became interchangeable parts. Today, human resources, i.e. people, are said to be important. One caution, however. In some management literature there is a concern that people could become a problem during periods of rapid change. The thesis is that some employees might be too loyal to their organization. (Scary huh?)

Most organizations today have supervisors, forepersons, or bosses. Frederick Herzberg's well-documented motivational research advises that there are two key dissatisfiers in most organizations: (1) company policy and administration and (2) supervision.

If you are a supervisor you must not take this revelation personally. You also need a laugh more than anyone but, you should recognize that, it is organizational ritual to "blame" or make fun of the first line supervisor. This is because the supervisor is the messenger of bad tidings—the one who must oversee(r) company policy and administration.

The words themselves provide us with humor. First of all a supervisor has two qualities: (1) the constant need to be super and (2) the person of great vision. A supervisor must be godlike and omniscient. We should not laugh at those attributes. We do.

Contrast this with the word subordinate. Sub is of course under, below, really inferior. Ordinary we know is commonplace. So if you are a subordinate you are below commonplace. You are in the same class as submarine, suburban, substitute, subtract, subcaliber, subgroup, and subhuman. All of these actually sound better than subordinate with the possible exception of subhuman.

Once again the *climate* (an *in* word) and *vision-* a maybe word) and *environment* (a safe word) have an impact on the role of supervisors. In larger organizations, supervisors move to new jobs at eighteen month intervals, apparently to keep employee juices flowing. Top management says it's for development of supervisors, but one has to think it's to keep employees on their toes. Why? No manager/supervisor/boss ever manages in the same manner (in spite of all the training). There are autocratic dictators often masked as benevolent. There are democratic leaders masked as empowerment coaches. There are free reign supervisors masked as being "out of the office today."

Supervisors have to be clever at passing on a lot of the flotsam and jetsam they get from top management in such a way that the troops do not revolt. By the same token, if supervisors relayed all the information they received from the rank and file to middle management or beyond, everyone would be fired.

Organizations: Zoo-like or For the Birds

Many organizations are like a zoo as in the expression: "This place is like a zoo."

They have drowsy lions. Bored. Yawning. Drowsy. They remind you of people on the job—people who have already retired on the job.

They include monkeys. None of the people in the office can hang by their tails (or even tales). Nevertheless every office has a swinger.

When you think of three blind persons trying to describe an elephant, can you think of groups in organizations where there might be different views of missions, visions, and objectives?

Many organizations also have giraffes. They can see what is going on no matter what. They read faxes upside down.

There are others. Penguins dress for success. The peacocks are worse, catching every style change. The foxes, all definitions from slinky to wily, are generally found in the office rather than the plant. Every night a maintenance person (read zoo keeper) comes in to clean it all up to be ready for the next day of business.

Other organizations include birds as in the expression: "This place is for the birds."

Here are species not limited to one organization:

The Goose Family: Great White Fronted Emperor

The Loon Family: Yellow-billed, Common

Marsh Ducks: American Widgeon (Is this the origin of the well-known product widgets?)

Boobies: Red footed, Blue footed

Sandpipers: White Rumped, Sharptail, Little Stint

Grouse: Ruffed

Cuckoo: Common

Chapter Five

Communications: Seedbed of Humor

When things go wrong or right or in-between it's all said to be the result of good/bad/indifferent communications between "they".

Maybe the message is inaccurate, too complex, outdated, incomplete, unpleasant, and/or disturbing. Look at those words for a moment. They offer the opportunity for anguish, but they also open the door for humor.

Then think about the sender. In today's organizational—and mostly hierarchical structure—the sender is often the boss or a staff person whose opinion "must be respected." Any chance for humor there?

Like an overflowing septic tank, all the stuff runs downhill to a receiver. His/her perspective at the bottom is where a great deal of potential humor resides. Humor exists everywhere in the communication chain.

Witness this story told by Dr. Joel Goodman, Director of the Humor Project:

> A businessman ordered flowers to be sent to the opening of his friend's new branch office. When the businessman got there, he was delighted to see a beautiful floral arrangement. However, he was more than distressed when he read the card that had accompanied the flowers—it read, "Rest in Peace."
>
> He made a beeline to the flower shop and immediately started chewing out the florist. After the shouting had subsided, the florist reassured him by saying, "Hey, don't worry! Just think... somewhere today in this city, someone was buried beneath some flowers that read, 'Good luck in your new location!'"

Memorandums From Top Management

Since so much communication appears to be top down, let's start with messages from top or middle management to the supervisor of the troops. These often take the form of memorandums that end up in electronic mail or in-baskets.

As an important urgency-breaker exercise (and there will be many more in this humor odyssey) one can take a memo from top management and rewrite it (humorously if you are now predisposed) into a thing of beauty for the troops.

With a little imagination the following memos from top management could be real. In each case there is an original memo, and a sample of a follow-up memo by a supervisor or middle manager. (If you want you could try your hand at writing your own follow up memo.)

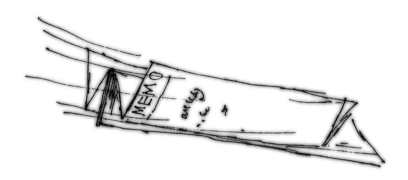

Memo # 1

From: Benefit Committee Chairman

To: Mid-managers

Subject: Preventive Health Measures

It is critically important for our organization to be lean and mean. We will discuss mean in a later memo, but for the moment we want to concentrate on lean.

Lean people make a good impression.

Lean people do not eat or drink to excess.

Lean people generally exercise.

Lean people take care of themselves.

To say the least, these are very desirable qualities and it would appear to bode well for the company. However, it appears that this is being done to excess. Many not so thin people have succumbed to the stress of competition with lean people and are eating in excess to take out their frustrations. This is running up the costs of our health plan.

Thin people are asked to continue to be lean but not to flaunt it. One way of doing this would be for thin people to pad their clothes.

Memorandum # 1 (Follow up)

From: Mid-managers

To: All Employees

Subject: Health Measures

Our human resources people tell us that we are spending too much for meals on our expense vouchers. From now on lean people will get fourteen cents per ounce allowance per meals—those overweight only seven cents an ounce. We trust that no one will pad their expenses. (Check the cafeteria or the benefit committee office for the appropriate weight chart.)

If you have any questions, consult your supervisor.

Memo # 2

From: Division Manager

To: Supervisors

Subject: Memorandums and Appraisals

First of all we want to compliment you on the quantity (and we're sure quality) of the memos that you're writing. This is by far the largest number of memos written since we have instituted the new appraisal plan.

It has come to our attention, however, that memos are being written at all hours of the day and night. Our human resources people who keep record of such things believe our twenty-four hour clock of memos is being skewed toward the later evening and early morning hours.

On the surface this would appear to be all right, but since our appraisal plan gives more credit for late night and early morning memos they distort overall results. (It is entirely possible some people have found a way to reverse clocks on their computers.)

Unless this stops, Human Resources will have to reexamine the appraisal plan. Once again, however, congratulations on the number of memos.

Memo # 2 (Follow-up)

From: Supervisor

To: Employees

Memo: Quantity of Memos:

Congratulations on the quantity of memos.

Because of a peculiarity of the appraisal plan, it appears we get more credit for memos written late at night and in the early morning hours.

We suggest that if you do have to work late it is apropos to write your memos at the end of the evening. The plan may be changed to better enable this, but until that happens, we can achieve better results by batching and sending all of our memos at night.

Memo # 3

From: Organizational Dynamics Headquarters

To: GD (General Distribution)

Subject: Acronyms

We have recently had some discussions about the use of Acronyms here at OD. For clarification purposes:

ASAP means as soon as persuaded

FYI means for your in-basket

FYE means frame your etchings

JIT means jammed in traffic

LIT means lost in transit

OJT means on-the-job-thinking (which is to be encouraged in several of our departments)

CC formerly was carbon copy…now means copious copies

Memo # 3 (Follow-up)

From: Employees at OD

To: Management of OD

Subject: AHAA

Acronyms Here Are Awful.

Memo # 4:

From: Top Management

To: Middle Managers

Subject: Communication Bottlenecks

A confidential survey conducted surreptitiously reveals that communication from top management down to middle management has been superb. Interestingly enough the communication up to middle management has been excellent.

The problem is that no messages are getting through middle management. Effective December fifteenth all middle managers will be let go.

Memo # 4 (Follow up)

To: Employees

From: First Level Supervisor

Subject: Turkeys

As in the past, top management has agreed to give all employees a turkey for the holiday season on December fifteenth. At the same time our middle managers will be leaving the firm.

Memo # 5

From: Network Control

To: Computer Stations

Subject: Dress Code at Home

Effective January 1, personnel who work from a work station in their homes will be fully dressed at all times.

This is because our new monitoring technology has video capability and headquarters has asked us to keep surveillance of you at all times.

Being scantily clad or wearing pajamas will no longer be acceptable even though our vice president/general manager has taken a personal interest in this activity.

Memo # 5 (Follow Up)

From: Mini-network control

To: Work stations

Subject: Dress Code

Re: Attached memo on dress code

On free-dress days at the home office, employees at home stations will be able to wear the normal pajama, bathrobes, and lighter wear on hot days. The vice-president wants to know when this happens because of his interests.

Two other things: (1) Please do not ask for a clothing allowance; and (2) please use discretion in allowing children to play at your work station. We are subject to child labor laws and the state people may suggest we pay your children for the time on camera.

Memo # 6

From: Accounting Dept.

To: Office Managers

Beginning July 1, we are assigning special cartoon access points on all copying machines and faxes in the business. This is to ensure that our paper costs are properly distributed by department.

The rationale for this is that certain departments are not getting the opportunity of good communication via cartoon distribution. We know informally that little real humor is going on in engineering and, we're sorry to say, not much in our department as well.

With CAPS (cartoon access points) we will have an accurate statistical device to ensure all departments get equal access to cartoons.

Memo # 6 (Follow up)

To: Office Managers

From: Group Manager

Subject: CAPS

The attached memo has reached me and it disturbs me. I feel that we should not do anything with this at this particular time because I believe the staff study from Accounting is not complete. To come up with a way of recording number of copies, distribution, etc., is totally insufficient. They will also need to explain the cartoons as well. Otherwise, certain departments, e.g., engineering will still be at a disadvantage. Do nothing about CAPS until you hear from me.

Often one becomes addicted to these kinds of memos. Further evidence can be found in Appendix A.

For your next interdepartmental or team meeting why not use the memo writing opportunity as an ice breaker? Who knows? You may be able to discover some underlying problems that get in the way of communication or effective management. However, don't expect people to laugh right away. They have become accustomed to so many "real life" ludicrous memos, they will assume the same for the crazy memos you create.

"Memos Happen" is an appropriate bumper stick to further clarify the role of memos in the organization world. If the climate is not right for you to take credit for memo creativity, leave an anonymous copy in every copy machine. There is no reason to thwart open communication and fast distribution.

Unfortunately, one does not see many humorous memos—those designed to communicate, give perspective, and entertain. So why shouldn't you do something about it? If, for example, you have a job responsibility associated with a computer network here is a possibility:

> "We regret that the computer network ("Bertha"-"Harold") went down this morning, causing disruption of your e-mail. This weekend our technical people will make the necessary corrections to block this happening again. Since the system at times generates anger and denial, our techs will be joined by a therapist."

> (Signed)   The Management.

E Mail

E-mail is the newest device for transmitting information to one another...and the newest for in-house humor. The e-mail messages sent to everyone in the organization are usually short and off the cuff. With a little imagination (and perhaps taking a few things out of context) you can have at least one and maybe several laughs a day.

Following are a few lifted from network broadcasts (along with asides):

"MARY SMITH IS LOCATED IN A TWENTY-THREE, NOT IN THE FIRESIDE ROOM AS INDICATED IN THE STAFF DIRECTORY." (ALL INDICATIONS ARE SHE COULDN'T STAND THE HEAT.)

"I AM LOOKING FOR SOMEONE'S BEACH HOUSE TO RENT FOR A SATURDAY NIGHT ONLY IN MAY OR JUNE FOR FIFTEEN PROFESSIONAL WOMEN." (YES, ALL THEIR HEALTH CARDS ARE CURRENT.)

"WE FIRST DIRECTED THE MESSAGE BELOW TO ADMINISTRATORS, BUT DECIDED WE REALLY WANT INPUT FROM FACULTY OR ANYONE WITH AN OPINION." (NOW THAT TELLS IT LIKE IT IS.)

"WE'D LIKE YOU TO JOIN US. WHY NOT GET YOUR FEET WET IN A WHOLE NEW ACTIVITY? IT'S SPRING! TIME FOR NEW THINGS. IT'LL HELP TAKE YOUR MIND OFF WHAT AILS YOU—AND ASSIST YOU IN PERSONAL AND PROFESSIONAL GROWTH AT THE SAME TIME. " (HOURLY RATES ARE AVAILABLE FOR THE HOT TUB.)

"A LADY FRIEND OF MIND HAS HAD HER HOUSE SOLD OUT FROM UNDER HER." (WE'RE NOT SURE WHY SHE WAS ON THE ROOF. RAISING IT?)

"THE SPRING NEWSLETTER IS DUE OUT IN MAY. ANYONE WHO HAS NEWS OF INTEREST ABOUT OUR WOMEN IS WELCOME TO SUBMIT INFORMATION." (IT MAY NOT BE PUBLISHABLE, BUT IT OUGHT TO BE GOOD READING.)

THE NEXT MEETING OF THE ACTIVE LEARNING COMMITTEE WILL BE HELD AT TWELVE NOON. (YOU CAN DO ANYTHING FOR AN HOUR.)

THE (BLANK) GROUP WILL HOST A BROWN BAG FORUM ON DEPRESSION IN THE SPRUCE ROOM. (THIS IS UPBEAT—IT COULD HAVE BEEN HELD IN THE BLUE ROOM.)

FREE TO FIRST CALLER: TWO FREE ROOM DIVIDERS. (SORRY, WE ALREADY HAVE TWO PEOPLE LIKE THAT IN THE OFFICE.)

SURPRISE VISITOR IN MY HOME! WE HAVE AN URGENT NEED FOR BABY CRIB, CHANGING TABLE, ETC. (INCIDENTALLY THE SURPRISE VISITOR LEFT ABOUT NINE MONTHS AGO.)

AS PART OF THE CELEBRATION OF EARTH DAY, THE PEACE AND CONFLICT AND ENGINEERING PROGRAMS ARE SPONSORING A FORUM THAT WILL ADDRESS THE USAGE AND RESTORATION OF THE COLUMBIA RIVER. (AT THE LUNCHEON SALMON WILL BE SERVED.)

ONE OF OUR INSTRUCTORS IS IN DIRE NEED OF A FILE CABINET. (SHOULD HAVE WHEELS SINCE HE IS ONLY TEMPORARY.)

IT'S THAT TIME OF YEAR AGAIN. WELCOME IN SPRING WITH THE EIGHTH ANNUAL SECRETARIES' BRIEFING CONFERENCE. (THIS WILL BE FOLLOWED BY A MORE INTERESTING DEBRIEFING SESSION IN THE SUMMER.)

More Communication Devices

Words Themselves

One of the greatest stack of paper assets that a worker can have is a loose-leaf funny file. Anything that you laugh at, or even smile about, is worth copying or cutting or writing down to put in your funny file. It doesn't have to be complicated. It could be words. Many are humorous in themselves. Here are but a few examples:

AARDVARK. NOW WHAT DOES THAT HAVE TO DO WITH WORK LIFE? ABSOLUTELY NOTHING. BUT WOULDN'T IT BE GREAT TO HAVE ONE AROUND TO CLEAN UP THE ANTS THAT CLEAN UP THE CRUMBS IN THE LUNCH ROOM?

ABSENT MINDED. THE IMPLICATION HERE IS THAT THIS IS ONLY A TEMPORARY EXPERIENCE. DO YOU KNOW SOMEONE WHOSE EYES GLAZE OVER EASILY?

ACCIDENT PRONE. SHE/HE LIES DOWN WAITING FOR ACCIDENTS TO HAPPEN?

AIR-HEAD. YES, BUT THERE MAY BE CONDUITS AVAILABLE FOR MOVING MESSAGES WITHOUT JUDGMENT. FOR EXAMPLES TRY MOST ANY CHAT GROUP ON THE INTERNET.

ARROGANT. STAND ALONE SUPERIORITY. (THIS IS WHY THIS PERSON OFTEN STANDS ALONE.)

AVARICIOUS. ENTIRE MARKETING DEPARTMENTS AND ALL SALES PEOPLE COULD BE FIRED IF THEY DIDN'T HAVE SOME OF THIS. BESIDES, THE WORD SOUNDS LIKE GOOD THINGS LIKE DELICIOUS AND NUTRITIOUS (RATHER THAN CRASS WORDS LIKE GREED).

BRAGGART. SINCE WE ARE MORE SOPHISTICATED, THIS IS AN ARCHAIC WORD. AS A REPLACEMENT WE HAVE BUMPER STICKERS THAT SAY SUCH THINGS AS: "I'M THE PROUD PARENT OF AN HONOR ROLL STUDENT." THE SEQUEL WILL BE "BRAINS ON BOARD." WHEN THE TEENAGER GETS A CAR HE CAN HAVE A BUMPER SIGN THAT READS: "MY FATHER, A SUCCESSFUL MANAGER, WAS PROMOTED AGAIN LAST WEEK."

BIGOTED. THERE CAN BE NOTHING FUNNY ABOUT SOMEONE WHO IS THIS WAY UNTIL YOU REALIZE THAT EVERYTHING THEY SAY IS FUNNY. DEFINITELY NO REQUIREMENT FOR "BRAINS ON BOARD."

BIRDBRAIN. IN MANY RESPECTS THIS IS DEGRADING AND IS NOT APPROPRIATE FOR USE IN THE OFFICE. (THERE ARE MANY BIRDS THAT HAVE DEMONSTRATED KEEN INTELLIGENCE.)

BONDED. IT IS THE IN WORD REPLACING STICKY WICKET; COMING UNGLUED IS UNACCEPTABLE.

BUSYBODY. MOST LIKELY THE OFFICE GOSSIP WHO TALKS ABOUT OTHER BODIES THAT ARE ALLEGED TO BE BUSY AT ALL HOURS.

CHEAP. A GREAT FUNNY WORD. ITS APPLICATION IN THE WORKPLACE IS UBIQUITOUS. FOR EXAMPLE, DO YOU KNOW SOMEONE WHO EATS HANDFULS OF CANDY FROM THE FREE STANDING CANDY DISH IN THE OFFICE? HE ALWAYS "FORGETS" TO BRING IN CANDY.

CHOPPED LIVER. A COMMON EXPRESSION OF A WIN/LOSE SITUATION IN THE WORKPLACE. EVEN THE WINNER LOSES (AT LEAST HIS LIVER) IF HE CELEBRATES BY DRINKING.

COMPLAINING. IS THERE SOMEONE IN YOUR OFFICE WHO COMPLAINS ABOUT EVERYTHING? SENSE OF FAIRNESS? ROOM TEMPERATURE? THE NEW BOY IN THE OFFICE? THE COMPUTER PROGRAM? THIS IS PROBABLY NOT ACCURATE ANYMORE FOR WE KNOW FOR A FACT THAT SHE HAS TRANSFERRED TO OUR OFFICE.

CURIOUS. THE GAME HERE IS HOW TO KEEP OVER CURIOUS PEOPLE FROM KNOWING ANYTHING. THIS IS PARTICULARLY USEFUL WHEN COMPETING DIRECTLY WITH THEM.

DING-A-LING. NO LONGER APPROPRIATE IN OFFICE WORK SITUATIONS. MOST OF THE PHONES HAVE DIFFERENT TONES THESE DAYS ANYWAY.

EASY. WHY IS IT SO EASY TO IRRITATE ALMOST EVERYONE?

EDGY. THIS IS WHAT HAPPENS TO EVERYONE IN THE OFFICE WHEN THE BOSS IS ON EDGE.

FREUDIAN SLIP. WE'RE ADVISED THAT THERE WAS A FREUD WHO WAS A DESIGNER OF WOMEN'S UNDERGARMENTS.

GROUCHY. THIS IS A GENDERLESS ATTRIBUTE IN THE OFFICE WITH THE RECENT MEDICAL DISCOVERY OF PMS.

HOLIER-THAN-THOU. THIS COMES WITH AGE. LOOK CLOSELY AROUND THE EYES. FEW LAUGH LINES AND PERMANENTLY ARCHED EYEBROWS ARE CHARACTERISTICS.

JEEPER'S CREEPERS. ARCHAIC. PERHAPS ACCEPTABLE FOR USE AS AN EXCLAMATION IN THE CHRYSLER ORGANIZATION.

KLUTZ. EVERY ORGANIZATION NEEDS ONE. THE RATIONALE HERE IS THAT EVERYONE IN THE ORGANIZATION CAN HAVE GREAT SELF ESTEEM IN HOW THEY LOOK, MOVE, AND ARTICULATE JUST BY COMPARING THEMSELVES WITH THE COMPANY KLUTZ. (DON'T FIRE HIM.)

MINCE MEAT. IN THE INTENSE CORPORATE WORLD IT IS BETTER TO BE THE CLEAVER THAN THE MEAT.

NARROW-MINDED. A VACANT TUNNEL BETWEEN THE LEFT AND RIGHT EARS.

NUDGE. A GENTLE APPLICATION OF THIS WORKS BETTER THAN A REPRIMAND. SIGNIFICANT OTHERS DO THIS WELL.

OVERSIGHT. THIS IS NOT UNCOMMON WHEN A BOSS IS LOOKING OVER YOUR WORK.

QUACK. PERHAPS ONE OF THE GREATEST EXAMPLES OF HUMOR IN A WORD. "IF IT SOUNDS LIKE A DUCK..." ANYWAY, IT IS NOW OBSOLETE FOR THE SINGULAR IS BEING REPLACED BY THE PLURAL. IN THE MEDICAL FIELD, FOR EXAMPLE, IT IS POSSIBLE TO HAVE GROUP QUACKERY.

RAUCOUS. AS IT SOUNDS: UNREFINED SWEARING.

SCREAMERS. IN THE BEST OF ORGANIZATIONS THIS WILL HAPPEN. SCREAMERS MUST BE KEPT AWAY FROM CUSTOMERS.

SIGNIFICANT OTHERS. THIS WORDING DISTINGUISHES PEOPLE FROM INSIGNIF-ICANT OTHERS.

TAG-A-LONG. IF THE BOSS STOPS TOO ABRUPTLY THIS CAN BE A REAL PROBLEM FOR SOME EMPLOYEES.

UNIVERSAL JOINT. MOST ORGANIZATIONS HAVE A FAVORITE BAR THEIR EMPLOY-EES PATRONIZE.

There are words that have a funny twist or generate a funny image to the mind. Think of funny town names for example: Walla Walla, Poughkeepsie, George, Stillwater, Amity, Seacaucus, Drain, Drift, Bend, Weed, Puyallup, Buffalo, and Boring.

How about names? (If you have one of them, then there is no humor in them at all.) Try George, Daffy, Dudley, Bella, Bunky, Pinky, Penelope, Able, Cain, Buddy, Billy, Benny, Clyde, Desiree, Douglas, Fierello... (Yes, Clyde is funny. It's the present tense of clod.)

People in the news. (Just thumb through any weekly magazine and pick out the current names.) They provide opportunities for late-night standup comics. Often these "beautiful" or "powerful" (read political) people have such an abundance of arrogance that they seem fair game. If they do not bring themselves down to size—and many do uncon-sciously—humor does the job. (They provide employment for political cartoonists.)

Once again words alone can communicate humor.

Acronyms and Jargon

In-house jargon and acronyms are a wonderful source for humor. To a new person coming into your organization, the vocabulary is almost impossible to understand. You can do something about it. Come up with some new meanings for them—not the real ones but plausible meanings. This will help put these important communications pieces in perspective.

Here are two well-known acronyms:

The first is ASAP which of course means as soon as possible. But when you ask people what that really means it could mean as soon as practical (or palatable), as stupidly as possible, or possibly all six are packed. (For you purists ASAP also means Academic and Social Anxiety Program, After Sale Assurance Program, Advanced Symbolic Artworks Program, and American Society For Adolescent Psychiatry.) The second is JIT. Yes, we have heard it means *just in time*. It could just as easily be a jerk is tiresome or junk in transit. By this time you know it really means jest in time.

So once again it is your turn. Here are some acronyms that need explanation. We're sure you will be far more creative than my efforts shown in Appendix B. Remember, in this harried climate of shortcuts and time savers, these acronyms really do exist in at least one organization. For example the acronym FEAR shown below has the following real world meaning: Field Engineering Assistance Request, Forfeiture Endangers American Rights, and/or Federal Employment Activity Report. This may be more than you wanted to know.

AFS	CAP
EFT	AP
FEAR	FIOR
ASAP	PDQ
TYFSK	ETA
CRT	MOM
SNAFU	VDT

FOB	TOAT
PIC	MAI
APAR	PEDS
IPR	FTE
PDO	PDI
TQC	PIG
DOS	RFQ
EEOC	CPM
RFP	PC
FCC	SEC
RFQ	CAP
CEO	PYA
TGIF	SOL
HAP	TLC
SOB	SOP
FYI	TQM

If you become stuck look at the appendix for some suggestions. It may trigger something that is considerably better. With the jargon and acronyms that exist at work, is there any wonder that new people look confused? That will all change now since you have had a chance to give new, meaningful explanations for these collections of letters. There is no reason new people should not know that ASAP means all shifts are procrastinating.

Playing Telephone

Let's play telephone. One of the great forms of communication is the one-on-one informal message that often starts at a coffee break. Gossip and weeds grow with surprisingly little nurturing.

In your next team meeting consider an ice breaker using this technique. The leader has a formal message that he reads and then passes on to the person orally and, of course, confidentially. The receiver then passes the message around to the person next to her and so on around the circle until the message gets to the person immediately to the left of the originator. It can be even better if you have two messages being circulated at the same time.

Compose your own messages. Here are a few workplace messages, however, to get you started:

Peter, Paul, and Pauline are new interns assigned to the hospital. Periodically they will, in addition to normal responsibilities, take a pathogenic view of the amount of patience we display with patients. There is indeed a pathology in the science of dealing with people requiring, of course, pathos and forbearance. Reports will be submitted.

And/or:

There were twenty-five guys standing around as the wheel spun off the hydraulic lift truck and catapulted into the office where Miss Jones was talking on the phone to Harry Forester explaining why his job wouldn't be done until Monday or perhaps this Friday at the earliest. She was narrowly missed. (And it went over her head as well.)

And/or:

Outside the bank a furtive looking character is nervously pacing back and forth. Inside, a man and a woman are approaching the teller; the woman is carrying a large black purse. The teller is looking at three men in a corner who are talking to a loan officer. The loan officer pushes a button underneath her desk, and automatically pictures are taken of the backs of the culprits.

And/or:

There is a new young woman in the office today. She is wearing a blue business suit and a maroon tie and carrying an attaché case. She is from the front office and, some say, is a special friend of Mr. Bigg, the president of the corporation. She is very knowledgeable about benefits. She has been promoted again, the third time in the last three years. She is thirty two. And/or:

The human resources vice-president announced that the We Can Do It firm headed by Ann Swenson received the bid to handle the training for the manufacturing arm of the organization. In explaining the bid he said she seemed to have more intimate knowledge than the other groups; she also said they could do the hands-on training right away. The reject group will be trained first.

Now, listen to the messages that came back and track them with the original message.

Marvelous! Once again the opportunity for communication can go astray because of the message. Add a sender with an opinion. Add a receiver who is cynical and another who is suspicious. It can be grim. Fortunately it can be funny as well.

Lest you think that our communication discussion is intellectually inadequate, let me now provide you a sampling of good, solid, intelligent, and bright writing:

Subject: Calculations

To: Employees

Accuracy and precision are attributes of prime significance and importance; they should not be taken lightly or obscured in the accumulation and amassment of raw statistical data. For this reason, use the scientific method in summing the data; the numbers should be added consecutively in sequential order.

1) 43, 819, 756, 428, 514

2) 223, 1601, 243, 306, 294

3) 1803, 620, 304, 223, 107

4) 312, 420, 607, 1725, 280

5) 606, 2520, 352, 431, 707

Although we could come up with a mode or median, it is only necessary to arrive at a statistical mean.

In reviewing random numbers of this sort it is imperative that raw data or even the averages not be considered of complete statistical value in matching the universe. For this reason will you now please take the statistical mean of the means.

Tabulate the raw numbers that could be said to be above the statistical mean and those below; this along with other data can be use in achieving the deviations from the mean.

The person who wrote this is certainly knowledgeable. These kinds of memos, often found in technical groups, have advanced degrees or studies written all over them.

Knowledge can be power. Knowledge displayed this way can be laughable, particularly when viewing the following alternative solution to the above problem:

"Please add the twenty-five random numbers above and come up with an average. How many of the numbers are above the average and how many are below?"

Any Number Will Do

We suspect that power, or imagined power, plays a role in many communications. It's considerably more important the higher you are in an organization. But if you do not yet have the credentials, we have located a formula that will enable you to be precocious, bright, and intellectual without the risk of having to say anything of substance.

Just think of a three digit number in Figure 4 from 000 to 999; than take the matching numbers from each group and come up with the matching phrase. Try the number 256 for example: Upgrade Customer Image. The phrase may not mean anything, but it sounds intelligent and unfortunately has a ring of familiarity. (It could have come from a graduate course in marketing.) More importantly, the phrase as well as the process is humorous. Go ahead. Try any three-digit number.

Figure 4

Any Number Will Do

Group 1	Group 2	Group 3
0 Study	0 Organizational	0 Competencies
1 Coordinate	1 Quality	1 Research
2 Upgrade	2 Program	2 Implications
3 Consolidate	3 Professional	3 Planning
4 Total	4 Leadership	4 Excellence
5 Review	5 Customer	5 Acceptance
6 Finalize	6 Differential	6 Image
7 Systematized	7 Decision Making	7 Improvement
8 Continuing	8 Innovative	8 Flexibility
9 Ongoing	9 Policy	9 Programming

See, there you are, you can be bright, pompous and funny—by the numbers.

More Fog—Public Relations Talk
a.k.a : "Employee Information"

If openness and candor exist at top management, there is little need for public relations people. In the real world, then, "public relations" exists as a strong career path for many, particularly in a field called "employee information."

It takes real skill and perhaps some cynicism to write good copy for employees and not say anything. Many in this career path drop out or become alcoholics. Since one's editors, the real editors, are top management, it becomes evident that this is the group for which to write. (Other employees will become adept in reading between the lines, or, what is more likely, won't read any of the messages at all.)

Here are some sentences we have extracted from a recent "all employee information" bulletin that demonstrates how far employee information has really come:

WE MUST DRAMATICALLY IMPROVE OUR RESPONSIVENESS WHILE SHARPLY REDUCING OUR COSTS" (TRANSLATION: WE ARE GOING TO ADD EMPLOYEES. RIGHT?)

MATCH THIS WITH "THE GATHERING STORM OF COMPETITION" AND THE NEED TO "TRANSFORM OUR BUSINESS." (TRANSFORMERS OFTEN GO OUT IN A STORM.)

"WE WILL ULTIMATELY DESIGN A SYSTEM THAT DOES NOT FAIL." (ULTIMATUM AND ULTIMATELY ARE ONLY SOUND ALIKE. OF COURSE.)

"WE WILL USE REENGINEERING TECHNIQUES TO DEVELOP ENTIRELY NEW WAYS OF SERVING THE CUSTOMER." (THIS WILL BE A REMIX OF HIGHER TECH, HIGHER AUTHORITY, AND NEW WAVE.)

"NEW PRODUCT AND SERVICE DELIVERY WILL BE UNIQUELY CONFIGURED TO SATISFY THE NEEDS OF EACH CUSTOMER. NEW CENTERS WILL BE NEWLY CONFIGURED." (CONFIGURED WILL BE DEFINED IN A FUTURE ALL-EMPLOY-EE BULLETIN ON GLOBAL COMPETITION. BY THE WAY, YOU MIGHT WANT TO BRUSH UP ON FOREIGN LANGUAGES.)

"WE MUST HAVE MORE CUSTOMER-FRIENDLY WAYS OF DOING BUSINESS AND BE MORE EMPLOYEE FRIENDLY AS WELL: FASTER, SIMPLER, AND MORE SAT-ISFYING." (WITH THOSE WE HAVE LEFT WE HOPE TO BE ON A FIRST NAME BASIS.)

Anyway, you can see what this communications can get you. Hopefully, only skepticism. If the reaction is deep cynicism then real humor is lost. For the health of the people who write these things, they must stand back and laugh at the process. In so doing there is hope that they can right (by writing) the situation in the future.

A workshop participant gives us a final thought on how a twist in communications helped relieve stress:

Indeed, I have seen laughter work miracles many times. There is no better way to lighten up a tense situation than to introduce humor into the mix.

I can recall an excellent example from a particularly tense situation with a previous employer. This was a small, high-risk, high-tech endeavor, and we had just run out of money. We were all huddled in a conference room trying to decide what our story to our investors was going to be. Despair had a secure grip on the group. For some sick reason, a Woody Allen movie scene popped into my head and I decided to share it with the group.

In a particular scene from his movie *Mid Summer Nights Sex Comedy*, Woody was asked what he did for a living. His reply: 'I'm an investment manager. I invest clients' money until it's all gone."

The room cracked up. Some almost to tears. We didn't improve our ad-hoc business plan much, but we all left for home a little less burdened by the problem.

Chapter Six

Customers Are People

The good news is that customers are people. The bad news is that customers are people. This concept is an abstraction in TQM (Total Quality Management) and TCQ (Total Customer Quagmire).

The following syllogism illustrates the point:

Those who give us money are worthwhile.

Our customers gives us money.

Therefore, our customers are worthwhile.

These transactions are important for highly complex reasons such as "market share" and "repeat business." Personable human relations are archaic. Some customers have people and humor skills like you. At the same time some customers have been long term members of the donkey species.

Helpful Tools For Working With Customers

To assure that this is an instructional tool, here are a few suggestions for improving direct customer service:

1. DON'T SCREAM ON THE FLOOR "I CAN'T TAKE THIS ANY MORE."

2. SAY "I'M SORRY WE CAN'T DO THAT. IT'S COMPANY POLICY YOU KNOW."

3. DON'T GIGGLE ABOUT THE SLIGHTLY SOILED, HEAVILY-USED CLOTHES THE CUSTOMER IS RETURNING.

4. DO NOT PUT YOUR FINGER IN AN ITCHING EAR. THEY WILL FEEL YOU'RE NOT LISTENING.

5. BE FOLKSY 1. TELL THEM HOW LONG YOU HAVE TO GO BEFORE YOU CAN RETIRE.

6. KEEP THE PLACE ORDERLY. THAT MEANS SIGNS ANNOUNCING "NO DRINKS," "NO STROLLERS," "NO FOOD," AND "NO SHOES-NO SERVICE" HAVE A PLACE.

7. HAVE YOUR FACE-TO-FACE CUSTOMER ANSWER ANY PHONE CALLS TO YOUR STATION WHILE YOU'RE WRAPPING THEIR PURCHASES.

8. DIFFERENTIATE REAL CUSTOMERS FROM PEOPLE IN OTHER DEPARTMENTS THAT SOMEBODY SAYS ARE YOUR CUSTOMERS.

9. BE FOLKSY 2. TELL THEM YOU WERE LOOKING FOR A JOB WHEN YOU CAME HERE.

10. HANDLE ALL PHONE CALLS WHEN SOMEONE COMES IN SAYING THEY ARE VERY ANGRY.

11. SMILE BROADLY WHEN YOU SAY "NO WAY."

12. BE MOST RESPONSIVE TO THE QUIETLY ANXIOUS FOR THEY ARE IN THE MOST NEED OF FINDING A REST ROOM.

Surviving the Ugly Customer

Kelly Foutts-Smith has had a few experiences with difficult customers. At one time she worked in a retail import store where she encountered less than enthusiastic customers, but they still came back time and time again. One customer in particular she recalled spent a lot of gas money and time to come into the store and complain that he had been overcharged a quarter the previous day. After a standard apologetic "what is the world coming to" spiel she gave him his hard-earned quarter. At that point the customer discovered that he had locked his only keys in his car and had to use the quarter to call a locksmith. She was more than happy to remind him that it was a good thing he had been overcharged.

In another situation her co-worker Eileen had the job of assisting a highly annoying couple. They had purchased a straw doll, about four inches tall, and wanted it wrapped and placed in a box. They were sending it all the way to Europe, they explained many times. She watched from under cover as Eileen wrapped this doll (retail price $2.99) for its long journey. Once wrapped the couple wanted to be sure (with their very own eyes) that the price tag had been removed. Eileen then unwrapped the doll. The tag had been removed. She again rewrapped the doll. Then the man said he thought he had heard the doll breaking and thought it in his best interest to have Eileen unwrap the doll and look for injuries. She unwrapped the doll once again. Nothing was broken.

Finally, she wrapped the doll a third time and taped the box shut. The wife then said to her husband, "Do you think the doll's too pretentious. Maybe a frog figure instead?" (Retail price $2.49). By the time they had left the store Eileen seemed beyond even trained professional help.

I grasped another of the dolls in question and handed it to Eileen. She looked quizzically at me for a moment and then a devilish grin caught her face. She chucked that doll as hard as she could where it was caught in a huge useless paper lantern hanging from the ceiling. It hangs there to this day as a tribute to alleviated stress.

There are unhappy customers everywhere. Hear this experience from a bank teller:

I was working in the drive-through. An elderly gentleman came through and asked to cash a rather large check. I kindly asked him for a bank card and that is what must have set him off. "You mean you don't know who I am? I have been banking here for three months and you don't know me yet? I hate you guys here. You are so rude. You are always changing people back here so it's no wonder that you don't know me."

Just to let you in on the background, this gentleman's account happened to be at another branch. He has only been through ours a couple of times. He finally threw me his card and he started in by telling me how rude I was, how dumb I am, and that I needed to go back to school. Partially biting my tongue, I told him that I was currently a junior at Portland State, and that going back to school would not be necessary.

I sometimes find the rudest customers funny. I never take things personally or never take offense to what they are directing at me. If I did I would probably have quit by now.

Try this philosophical view of customer service by a governmental employee:

Teamwork has high value when you are in a business like vehicle and driver licensing, where "the customer is almost never right" and he would not choose to come at all if the law did not insist. Humor relieves tension and puts things in perspective. Processing complex transactions and dealing with difficult customers are bearable when you know the team is on your side and you can laugh together later.

Customer Service—the Good Guys

There are "good customers" everywhere. A workshop participant relates this experience:

Many years ago when I first started in the food service business, I was a cocktail waitress at a small quaint hotel. My shift was during the "happy hour" which was popular at that time. During this time period drinks came in the form of doubles which means they were twice as large as normal.

I worked the back section of the room on this particular evening. It was very busy so I did not see this certain group of people arrive. However, as I approached the table I could tell that there was something unusual about this group.

During my introduction and greeting of these patrons I realized they were blind. Upon further investigation it was made known to me that one man was sighted. I took their order and went to the bar to collect and return their drinks to them. They remained throughout "happy hour" and seemed to be having a great time. I returned to the table to give last call. Going around the table I asked each guest for their order. When I got to the sighted man he hesitated for a short while as if pondering whether to order another. Then I heard the blind man next to him say "'It's okay, John, have another drink. Remember I'm driving."

Contrary to a previous story there is hope for humor and laughter in banks.

Listen to the following by a teller:

People take their money very seriously, so I was keenly aware of the sensitivity of my customers. I know there could be ways of humanizing or reducing the stress of financial transactions and keeping the customer confidence in our institution intact. It would take some finesse, tactfulness, and most important, letting the customer know that the teller was their friend.

As I decided to try some different ways of easing the tension, I learned quickly that if I sincerely expressed an interest in them and spoke their name they would more easily respond and smile. After a few times through the drive-up, with snatches of conversation, I became acquainted with more of my customers. Then opportunities to create a humorous situation began to develop.

A customer arrived at my window at the drive-up and I could tell he was quite frustrated. He put his transaction in the drawer, commented apologetically that it was a very messed up deposit slip, and would I be able to understand what he wanted. Quickly, but seriously, I told him he was in luck because we were running a ten minute special on messed up deposit slips. He was quite astonished, then laughed heartily when he realized it was a joke. He commented that he'd watch for the ten minute specials.

Another way we have of making humor in the work place is by treating our customers' dogs to dog bones when they come through the drive-up. The dogs remember their treat and really get excited as their owner pulls up to the window. Not only are the owners tickled, but other customers enjoy seeing the antics of the dogs.

Quite a few of our customer know that we really like peanut M&Ms, Hershey kisses, and diet Pepsi, especially on busy days. Some days we say that the bank runs on chocolate energy. Our customers frequently drop off treats for us. When these little gestures of friendliness happen, we are no longer just a teller in the window and the customer is no longer just someone in the car.

Chapter Seven

Having Fun In Your Organization

It is now moment of truth time, dealing with your denials about humor where you work.

Humor does exist, although advance information suggests that you will have to be resourceful to find it, nurture it, and let it change your life. For you, this chapter alone will be worth the purchase of the book. (The price is too low, anyway, don't you think?)

There are other organizations where humor and fun have come together, almost as a surprise. A workshop participant makes this observation:

One of the greatest times I had at work was the first year the implementation staff was invited to join the sales force in the fun portion of their annual sales meetings. There had always been a rift between sales and implementation because of many perceived differences in each others' jobs.

Implementation felt they were expected to perform miracles by giving customers what sales had promised. Implementation felt they often were the reason a customer bought more software, but sales got the commission. Sales felt that implementation people had an easier life because they only had to make one trip in any given week, while sales could be in ten different cities in a five day period.

The wall between the two staffs was growing thicker, wider, and higher. The yearly sales meeting was five days long, with two afternoons off for fun outings as a group. Management decided the in-fighting had gone on long enough and something needed to be done.

It was decided, unknown to either sales or implementation, that all implementers would be in town at least one of those afternoons and would be invited on the spur of the moment to join the golf outing or the picnic/boat ride outing on the lake. The golf outing was first, and though several of the implementers were not golfers, they were invited to drive carts, partner up with a golfer, and hit a few shots, or just wait at the 19th hole for everyone to come in.

Everyone had a great time.

Many barriers were broken down, and some changes of attitude were obvious in a very short amount to time. The implementers were invited to the picnic, and every one of them eagerly accepted. I found out later that only one manager believed this would work, but he had enough influence to make it happen. Others were holding their breath, waiting for a major fight to take place on the golf course. Since it worked out so well, it became an annual event. And problems between the two departments have been relatively easy to work out since, without management involvement at all.

Discovering fun in an organization where tension dominates is exciting. What about being in a "bought out" organization? Kacie Christie relates this story:

Our company was purchased by a company from San Jose, California. This took most of us by surprise and caused a great deal of stress for all of my co-workers. There were rumors about a so-called "house cleaning" and no one felt secure in his or her position because of the uncertainty involved with this new arrangement.

Many of our familiar procedures were changed, but we were not offered the guidance or leadership necessary to incorporate these new objectives. Every time we made an attempt to clarify a situation we would only become more confused.

On the way to the meeting, I noticed the staff's defeated body language. We walked slowly, dragging our feet, with our heads hung low. Negative, unpleasant murmuring echoed through the halls. I heard one person say: "What are they going to do to us now?"

As we entered the meeting room and were scanning the room for an appropriate hiding spot, we were instructed to grab a bag out of the large cardboard box positioned in the center of the room. This caused a reaction of curiosity and suspicion. I approached the oversized box and noticed it was full of small brown paper bags that had been tightly folded and stapled shut. I picked one out of the deep center, confident I had made the right selection—whatever that was—and quickly returned to my seat. As I looked around, I noticed that everyone had placed the bags on the table in front of them and was reluctant to peek inside. I knew they wanted to.

Tammy, the trouble-shooter, called our attention and informed us that we were having "a-pick-your-nose-kind-of-meeting." Some of the staff chuckled quietly but many had a veil of confusion drape their faces. "What is she talking about?"

Before the meeting could begin we were instructed to open our chosen treasures. As we opened the bags we discovered noses of every shape, size, and color. There were fish, rhino, lizard, dinosaur, bird, chicken, cow, and even pig noses. They were made of bright colorful plastic and had an elastic band attached so we could wear them snugly over our faces.

The tension dissipated; we all laughed at each other's choices. We even noticed how appropriate some of the choices were. I sat with a bright pink pig's nose that had two huge nostril holes, unable to ridicule anyone on choice. It was tough to look at your neighbor without bursting out in laughter. We took group pictures with our noses on.

Although I do not recall the topic of that meeting, I do have a lasting impression of how successful that humorous tactic was in relieving the tension in that room. She was responsible for giving us some important information that day, but also realized how frustrated the staff was. Her use of humor in lightening the mood was very effective. It did not solve all of our problems, nor was it intended to, but that meeting made for an enjoyable experience in what had been a disastrous situation.

If humor exists in organizations going through painful transitions, then there can be no doubt that your organization is brimming with potential humor.

Time for reality therapy?

Okay. The word is out about your boss. Humor is not going to work everywhere overnight, particularly if the CEO, manager, boss, whoever, in your organization, is rigid, intense or driven. In these circumstances your appearance as a stand-up comic could easily get you back to Chapter three learning how to interview for a new job.

We have a secret.

Answer this question. What does the boss want?

Is it quality? Improved market share? Customer loyalty? Purse strings instead of heart strings? Once you determine what it is that turns on the boss, you can proceed to produce it in ways that are fun.

Say, for discussion purposes, it is quality of product or service. (How could you go wrong with something like that?) Your job is to get everyone in your organization to think in terms of improved quality, and you are going to look for something called continuous improvement.

So you put together a low-key campaign in your group called "Think Small." This means two things: (1) look at the little things on the product and/or service that need improvement, and (2) think like the little child in you, looking for creative free expression.

Then go for it. Look for ways to measure improvement.

Promote it with silly posters. Fun begins.

Give a small award for every idea and something extra when it is implemented. Celebrate it! Have fun. Make up small plays about the ideas. Ice cream bash breaks for recognition are a possibility.

When the improved results are in, show the boss what this program is doing to meet her objectives. Let her know that the extra fun time is paying off in increased quality. (Inform her that reject rates are going down, customers are happier, or the toggle switches aren't breaking, etc.)

The key to introducing humor and laughter where you are is to first celebrate organizational successes—successes that will improve the bottom line. Even the toughest boss will understand that and give approval. Be sure to include him in the celebration, and if useful, say something like this: "This would never have happened without the strong support of our enlightened management." (We suggest you don't gag when you say this.)

Once you have had some successes then you can look for ways to expand having fun. One way of including other groups is to provide special awards for the people who have given support to your organization above and beyond the call of duty. More awards. More prizes.

Perhaps the greatest result of all is the new open communications that come from such activities. What we are saying is: "If we can laugh and have fun you can too." The climate is there to talk openly—to develop trust. Revisiting Maslow, social needs are important; one could reasonably expect that more people satisfy these needs in the work place.

If you want more fun and less stress then look for other spot opportunities for fun. Celebration of birthdays. Potlucks for people. There are a number of occasions you could celebrate:

THE FORMATION OF THE INTERNAL REVENUE SERVICE.

THE DAY OSHA FOUND YOU WERE DOING SOMETHING RIGHT.

THE DAY OF RUNS. (STOCKINGS OR THE ANNIVERSARY OF THE THREE LEGGED RACES AT THE COMPANY PICNIC.)

BREAK UP OF THE USSR AND ITS IMPACT ON PRODUCT DELIVERY.

If you get a hole in one sock do you throw the other one away? Of course not. Celebrate two-socks day. Everyone will be required to wear two different socks to work. (At a bank have a banner suggesting to customers that they may not want to put all their money in one sock. "Open a second sock account with us so you can save for that special day when you need to buy a matching pair.")

What other kind of openness can you celebrate? How about a tailgate party in the parking lot for the people who helped the sales force meet their quotas?

Why not have Mini-Olympics as stress breakers: paper clip throws, archery with rubber bands, draw the boss contest, computer bits per minute contest, network solitaire contests, pin the tail on your favorite politician, brainstorm uses of electronic mail, standing push ups, standing broad jump, and copy machine adeptness (the number of sheets without a jam).

How about a "spin the bottle" meeting. Everyone gets candy kisses. The object is to have all participants suggest ways of eliminating bottlenecks at work. When the bottle points to you, you have to come up with a bottleneck and a suggestion or two for remedying it. The penalty for not doing it is give up some of your candy kisses to other participants. (It is possible to go too far with this idea. If the boss is the bottleneck, get another idea.)

How about retired employee parties? Include them in what you are doing, and celebrate their importance in getting you where you are. Celebrate the long term workers as well. Why not let people know we appreciate loyalty and are pleased to have them around. Have fun. It would be a fantastic departure from what is happening today in many organizations. (Be careful, however, of shock.)

Have impromptu videos. Abbott and Costello's: *Who's On First,* John Cleese's *Meeting, Bloody Meetings* and C.W. Metcalf's *Humor, Risk, and Change* come to mind as classics. You can intellectualize communications by talking about "what is happening to it" but you don't need to. Taking this kind of video break at a serious meeting may be just what the organization needs.

There may be opportunities for intramural sports after work: softball, basketball, ping pong, checkers, bingo, soccer, or dollar poker. There may also be opportunities for fun (and work) in cleaning up beaches, clearing a trail, improving a playground, trimming bushes, or promoting a good cause with a fun stroll.

Dress down. If you're not taking advantage of Halloween at the office you're missing a real bet. Let people be people. Would you rather do business with stuffed shirts or a goblin or witch at the teller's window on Halloween.

And think about Christmas. Think about the long lines at post offices. Does it help when the postal service people are wearing red Santa Claus hats? Yes. They are human and trying to be Santa's helpers and somehow the service is, or seems, better. (Generally this innovation comes from postal employees who purchased hats for their peers.)

Encourage commercial cartoon calendars.

In addition, consider these creative ideas for a large office calendar (with entries in crayon):

WHAT HAPPENED THIS DAY IN CORPORATE HISTORY. (TO DO THIS DIG UP OLD MEMOS.)

HOROSCOPE.

SONG FOR THE DAY.

THOUGHT FOR THE BOSS.

GREAT EXCUSES IN BUSINESS HISTORY.

GREAT COMEBACKS IN HISTORY.

A LIST OF CLEVER SAYINGS FROM YOUR MOTHER.

A LIST OF CLEVER THOUGHTS FROM HEADQUARTERS. (260 THOUGHTS—
ONE FOR EACH BUSINESS DAY—MIGHT BE A REAL TEST.)

Have a cartoon of the day on your bulletin board. If you have room for all those posted, unread federal laws you must have room for cartoons. Great sources for business humor, cartoons, and/or jokes include the *New Yorker, Readers Digest, Newsweek, Fortune, "Salt and Pepper"* in the *Wall Street Journal,* the periodical *Laughing Matters,* and any publication that features Dilbert.

Celebrations

Celebrations for customers. Baseball caps or T-shirts with customer logos could be distributed to those companies that have purchased your product or service for over ten years. (Involve as many people in the several organizations as possible.)

Smile of the month award for employees. You could have a certificate that reads: "You've earned the Smile of the Month award here at Excalibur. You do not have to say 'have a good day' to customers for the next thirty days." (Of course you will have to use a substitute expression such as "Did you find everything okay?")

Why not celebrate the patience of employees? Of customers? Of suppliers? (The Just in Time award would be appropriate for suppliers "who cared" and understood the needs of your business.)

How about an award for the employee who quietly makes mole hills out of mountains?

How about awards for participation on teams: most friendly, most humorous, ability to communicate and open up, most likely to admit when he or she is wrong, least complainer, the expediter, the most analytical, etc., until every one on the team is recognized.

Do you have an award for those customers who walked the extra mile to get to you? (If you have a customer in Melbourne why not have a "down under" award?) How about the most forgiving customer? The most appreciative?

In grocery retail why not have the "funniest customer" award for people who make you laugh—a sticker that entitles them to a stock of celery, dog bones, or a quarter pound of filberts (in addition to a gift certificate.)

The "Six billion people award" might be appropriate. This is what the world population would award if they knew about the employee's contribution.

Add a "humor cup" or plaque in the same gallery as the company sports trophies, for the person "who reduced stress and made this a better place to work." (This might be a rotating trophy.)

How about a celebration for the new employees in the organization? It could just be a ccy (cookie, coffee, and yogurt) party welcoming new people. No one could attend unless they told something unusual about themselves. (e.g., "Before coming here, I dealt with a queen. I was a beekeeper in Northern Idaho.")

Headlines—A Natural

You will need to reserve some space on your company bulletin boards for headlines from your local press. Newspaper headline writers take courses in advertising and biology. Most headlines are designed to get your attention; many are funny in themselves. You can make all headlines funny with an added comment about the subject.

See some recent headlines complete with commentary in Figure 7.

Figure 7:

"Some City Workers May Be Axed"
(We know it is a little hard to fire government employees, but this is a bit drastic isn't it?)

"Super Star Shows Strain Over Suit"
(If you had a suit that fit that tight you might show stress as well.)

"Apple Comes Down Off Its High Horse"
(An apple doesn't fall very far from the tree...but a horse?)

"Vikings Plunder Denver"
(We thought the Swedes were more civilized.)

"Season Opener Catches a Thief"
(Is this a big deal about a stolen base?)

"Many Dive Into Insurance Pool"
(Sink or swim with limited coverage.)

"Some Truckers Pull Off the Road"
(They were caught driving the posted speed.)

"Getting Up is Riskier Than Sexual Activity"
(What a way to go.)

"Salad Dressing Label Causes Stir in Washington"
(This is great all by itself. It has a nice toss to it.)

"Florida Authorities Hold Their Breath About Winter Tourism"
(Is this an alternative to term limitation?)

"Chicago Will Have To Reach Deep Down Now"
(They are out of the loop again.)

"Advanced Breed of Executives Remain in Perpetual Motion."
(Another spin is coming for the troops.)

"Passion Slips Away as Liberal Justices Leave"
(But at their age it was a source of embarrassment to us anyway.)

"Library May Be Shelved at Old State Building"
(Politicians have determined they no longer require libraries to compose sound bites.)

"Ten GOP Lawmakers May Defect"
(There are reported to be some defects on the other side of the aisle as well.)

"Bicyclists Suffers Injuries After Running Into Patrol Car"
(We received this information from a police department spokesperson.)

"Banks Rake in Cash From Bounced Checks"
(Rubber turns to gold.)

"LA Woman May Be Charged With Castration"
(We are going to leave this unkind cut alone.)

Ann Landers: "You Can't Equate Desire to Smoke With Sex Urge"
(Neither are permitted in the building.)

This wonderful source has been barely tapped. It is possible that you will have to increase the budget for bulletin boards. On every bulletin board there has to be room for the baby picture contest you are going to have. (Can't you just imagine what your boss looked like as a baby?) Also you will have to have room for the outrageous post cards your department will receive from employees on vacation. It will be a humor policy requirement that everyone sends one.

Signs Everywhere

There is humor everywhere you walk. All you have to do is look and see with the eye of a comic. Check out signs, notices, and bulletin boards. Consider the following found in a college student center:

Automatic Caution Door (If you were trying to learn English what would this mean to you?)

See Dawn in Counseling If you Have Questions (She gets there early.)

Cooperative Education (It's refreshing to have something like this in an uncooperative education world.)

Please Call the Office Before Arriving (If you've already arrived feel free to ignore this.)

General Job Placement (Specialists must find jobs on their own.)

Rest Rooms (If this is true do women get more rest than men? Clearly there is a need for a better designation such as bath rooms.)

Used History—1914 to Present (It is possible that it may be repeated again next term.)

Jam Packed Hour of Information (Please put your brown bags in the garbage after lunch.)

Colleges with MSDS Manual located in _____ (If you don't find it there, someone must have it.)

Mom, do it While the Kids are in School (Presumably this note on the bulletin board had reference to attending classes.)

Attention: Parking Permits now Required for all Students this Term (This was posted on the door of every public access room, including the rest rooms.)

Within five minutes of where you are there are funny things like this around you. All you have to do is look, see, distort, and laugh.

Go out on the streets or into the stores. You could save a lot of money and time by bringing in signs that have applications for your organization.

Here are just a few:

No Loitering (Put this near the coffee pot.)

Closed (Put this on your desk when you don't want to be disturbed.)

Help Wanted (Do not even respond when your sarcastic boss puts this up somewhere.)

One Way (Let people know you have an opinion.)

This Area Protected by Alarm System (Put this by the person most likely to scream when there is tension in the office.)

Ground floor (Tape to the surface of the first floor.)

If you Lived Here you Would be Home now (Place anywhere. With the increase in work hours most people think they do live "here.")

Day and Night Teller (We can place this at any location where gossip is transmitted. If your company has a cafeteria this is the right place.)

Pressure Washing (Put this near the shower in the plant. To alleviate the pressure in the future, women will get separate showers.)

Turn on Lights (This sign is in the entry hall for the building. This is the first instruction in the new employee guidebook.)

Yes, We're Open (Although this is on the boss's door, don't enter until you determine his mood.)

Tunnel (If you have a planning department post this sign near by as a hint that this would be appropriate in looking for another vision.)

No Right Turn (On your desk. If someone asks the meaning you can just say that it is a reminder that you will be blamed no matter what decision you make.)

Self Service (Do your own copying.)

Free Checking (Put this sign in the lead person's office or quality control.)

Dead End (Put this on a closet door. The curious will open the door every time.)

Play Here (This will be the code word to remind you to play solitaire on your computer when you are about to lose your mind.)

Copies 5 Cents each (Place on all copy machines. This will be a new revenue source for the business.)

Space Available (Entrance to your floor. Ignore. This is your employer again, trying to get you to work harder.)

Please Do Not Take Unpaid for Merchandise Into Rest Rooms (Since so many clothes are purchased on credit, this will most certainly cut down on the use of rest rooms at work, saving the company thousands of dollars in towels, toilet tissue, and water bills.)

Meetings That Work

Are meetings perceived to be boring in your organization? Do people daydream, doodle, and doze in meetings? Do some depart early? What should you do? Introduce laughter, of course, with some of the techniques suggested in this book.

However, here's one additional secret: put thought-provoking items next to the last item on the agenda. (Adjournment is the last item). People will race through other items on the agenda to get to something meaningful, saving valuable time that could be used more efficiently at the coffee bar. The bottom line will also improve as many practical suggestions will be offered.

Here is the short list of great agenda items (along with potential practical responses) to spread out over a series of meetings.

Elevator Courtesy

People are either looking up or bowing their heads. They are praying. Silence is important.

Do not say ding at every stop.

Do not say who did that?

Rationale for a Two Hour Lunch

Lunch hours at most restaurants are posted 11 A.M. to 1 P.M.

There are not enough good reasons for a three hour lunch.

Required for shopping and other stress reducing activities.

Customer Rapport

Say "that's a point of view" and move on to the next customer.

Suggest selected customers can find hip waders across the mall.

When things get hot say "I used to deliver mail."

New Areas of Study for Human Resources Department

Do you have a forwarding address for Charlie's form? He's no longer here. He died three years ago.

New ideas for desk safety.

The need for an automatic teller machine in rest rooms.

Meeting Stimulators

Stand up and perform "head and shoulders and knees and toes."

Automatic nudges every ten minutes. (This is the equivalent to automatic save in word processing.)

Rotate showing of home videos.

Inventing Interesting e-mail Messages

Turn off your computer and get to work.

Clean up your own files. Your mother doesn't work here.

Sharon came back to the office today; she is wearing red polka dot bikini underwear under her white stretch pants.

Creative Voice Mail Messages

I'll be back. I'm mowing the lawn due to outplacement of our maintenance people.

If you really need help lie. Tell the operator you don't have a touch-tone telephone.

If you must leave a message do it before the tone.

Things to Say to Children When They Call in Fighting

This can't be my sweet lovable children. You must have the wrong number. My kids would never call and interrupt my work day over dirty dishes.

Sorry little boy. This is not your mommy. This is her voice mail and she says you had better shape up.

No hables ingles.

If you are fortunate enough to be able to lead meetings try the above. People will demand the opportunity of attending your meetings.

Laughing at Ourselves and the Situations

Certainly the most effective device for nurturing humor at work is to look for it in ourselves.

Ginger Abel relates this story:

> The value of humor in the workplace was never more apparent to me than on my thirtieth birthday. My personal life was in turmoil and I looked to my work as, among other things, a way to escape. When I arrived at work the morning of my birthday I found black balloons tied to my chair, a Happy Birthday banner decorated with tombstones, and a morose-looking cake with spots of black frosting that turned our teeth black. That day will always be remembered as one of the very few hilariously happy days occurring during that otherwise difficult time.

Encourage those people who lend support and generate humor for the group. Here is a description of two such people by a peer:

> One worker organizes all the new employee, going away, holiday, and 'just because' potlucks. When she married we had lots of fun sneaking around to collect money for a gift, sign a card, wrap presents, and put on a potluck for her. It was a way of recognizing her contribution to the team, and we enjoyed surprising the surpriser.

> Another worker, a positive thinker with a sense of humor, brings a quote of the day. Handwritten on a 'post-it' note and

stuck to the lunchroom door, it is seen by everyone. It takes a couple of minutes each day for her to brighten everyone's day with a bit of truth and humor.

Jodi Syverson tells this story on herself:

As a computer operator of a mainframe system, I am one of two operators responsible for all aspects of insurance activity being printed and/or transmitted to our home office. Additionally, I am also required to keep our regional network system up and operating properly, including, but not limited to, cabling, fixing terminals and keyboard problems, and configuring pieces of equipment.

One morning I was the only person in our department of three. Network calls started coming in by what seems like the hundreds. I gathered all the information and proceeded to check the equipment. Nothing I did would bring the network system up. Within the next half-hour, our home office technicians and the regional manager as well as at least half of the building's other managers and supervisors were involved.

While I was on the phone to our home office technicians, I noticed that the power strip in which several of the controllers were plugged into was off. Can you believe it? All I needed to do was flip the switch. Oh, did I feel stupid. And the worst part about it was that I was responsible for calling everyone back to tell them that they should be up in approximately ten minutes and wouldn't you know it, everyone wanted to know what was the problem. How embarrassing.

After what I thought was all said and done, an incoming fax arrived just for me from our counterpart in home office (which should never have known about this problem). Word travels fast. The fax featured a cartoon showing the exact situation—the cord out—with two people bending over the computer, the caption reading: "I tried everything Ted. I just can't figure out what the problem could be…do you think we need a consultant?"

The fax made light of my bad situation and made me feel just a little bit better; now I could laugh at just how simple this huge problem was.

One more time: don't overlook the greatest opportunity for humor in your organization—you. Laugh at yourself and it will be contagious. A very close friend of ours is an attorney. He has a large porcelain shark sitting on the side of his desk. What do you think? Does that help him or hurt him with clients?

Finally, if you were a consultant what would you recommend to your organization to open communications, reduce stress, problem solve, and have fun?

Good! You're hired.

Chapter Eight

It's Creative

Creativity and humor have a strong connection. It's well documented. The only question might be, which is subordinate to the other.

Arthur Koestler says there are three domains of creativity:

Artistic originality (which he calls the "ah" reaction);

Scientific discovery (the "aha" reaction);

Comic inspiration (the "haha" reaction).

He defines creative acts as the combination of previously unrelated structures in such a way that you get more out of the emergent whole than you have put in. In the particular case of humor, according to Koestler, the interaction causes us "to perceive the situation in two self-consistent but habitually incompatible frames of reference."

The joke teller typically starts a logical chain of events. The punch line then sharply cuts across the chain with a totally unexpected line. The tension developed in the first line is therefore shown to be a put-on, and with its release the audience laughs.

This is even more true with situational humor. As an audience we're clearly not aware of being "set-up" with a first line. Most of the time the author of instant humor isn't aware of what is coming either. Situational humor is often funnier than jokes for precisely this reason.

Listen to a group of people brainstorm anything. Invariably you will hear much laughter as people let themselves go and come up with as many things as they can to help solve the problem. It is usually the unexpected that creates the opportunities for new services and products.

Brainstorming

Next time as an urgency breaker or warm-up for a group meeting brainstorm uses for a wooden bucket.

Here are a few possibilities:

YOU CAN KICK THE BUCKET

YOU CAN CARRY ANYTHING

YOU CAN BUILD A FIRE

YOU CAN SMOKE THE WOOD

SIT ON IT

HAVE A POTTED PLANT

MAKE KINDLING

CHEW ON THE SPLINTERS

USE FOR A HAT

USE FOR LAMPSHADE

PROVIDE SHADE FOR A SQUIRREL

BIRDBATH

TROUGH FOR STRAY DOGS

MAKE LINCOLN LOGS

PROVIDE STEPS FOR A LADDER

A BASKETBALL HOOP

HANGING PLANT

TRAP FOR BIRDS AND CHIPMUNKS

PLACE TO HIDE LIQUOR FROM THE RELATIVES

WASTE BASKET

MATCH WITH ANOTHER WOOD BUCKET AND MAKE A BARREL

DRUM

TOM TOM

THROW ON BONFIRE FOR THE HOMECOMING OF RETIREES

SNOWSHOES

XYLOPHONE BOARDS

RECYCLE INTO COMPUTER PAPER

PUPPET STAGE

SMOKESTACK FOR A TREE HOUSE

DOG HOUSE FOR A CHIHUAHUA

In this process we are getting as many ideas out as possible, and, at this point, we are not judging them. Laughter is the bonus.

Tools for Creativity

In pursuing creativity here are some strategies that work:

USE FREE ASSOCIATION. (IN RESPONSE TO "REJECT" YOU MIGHT SAY "RATE"; AT LEAST MANUFACTURING PEOPLE WOULD RELATE.)

THE SECRET HERE IS TO RESPOND QUICKLY, GIVING YOUR MIND FREE REIN.

LOOK FOR THE UNUSUAL. AFTER YOU HAVE COME UP WITH THE USUAL RESPONSES, FOR EXAMPLE MAGAZINE RACK, FLOWER POT, CARRYING WATER, ETC., IN USES FOR WOODEN BUCKET ABOVE, THEN FORCE YOURSELF TO LOOK AT THE CRAZY THINGS—THE ABNORMAL.

LOOK FOR ANALOGIES. STEAL IDEAS FROM OTHER INDUSTRIES, BUSINESS-ES, AND ORGANIZATIONS.

LOOK AT PROCESSES AND IDEAS IN OTHER ORGANIZATIONS THAT YOU COULD ADAPT. LOOK FOR THINGS THAT DO NOT WORK, (OTHER THAN FELLOW EMPLOYEES).

Stating the Problem

The proper statement of a problem is the key to solving it. If you do not know where you are going every piece of black top will take you there.

The secret is to think of at least five ways of stating the problem in an effort to select the best one.

Here are several to start with:

How can we get our organization to lighten up? and/or

How can we persuade the boss to take a sabbatical?

How can we show that our fun loving antics increase market share?

How can we darken everything else so by comparison we look light?

How can we get to the point where we do not shoot the messenger?

How can we laugh at ourselves to facilitate openness and caring?

How can we get men and women to work together?

How can we reinstate the wink and the smile without instigating a sexual harassment suit?

How can we get women to talk in "bullets" and men in relationships?

How do we clearly explain to men that the nod has unique meanings to men and women?

How can they "do lunch" without it becoming a problem?

How can we integrate men into the process of putting on organization potlucks?

What can we expect by the year 2010?

How will we know if we will be politically correct by the year 2010?

Will the years 2000-2009 be the zero decade?

How can we learn to be interactive with our computers without losing our identities?

Where will the right brain be by the year 2010?

What will the baby bust generation do to the boomers by the year 2010?

It is not intended that every problem has a humor twist, but introducing thoughts from the humor path aid and abet creativity and the creative process does the same thing for humor.

Random Words

Here is a great tool for getting another viewpoint. Simply, on a random basis, open your dictionary and pick the fifth word you see. Then do it again on other pages. I did it twenty-three times. (Tearing pages out of your dictionary to insure pure sampling is probably not a requirement unless you are an engineer.)

Here's how it works. First indicate a problem. Then randomly select words and see what bearing that word or concept has on the problem.

Here are a couple of examples:

Problem: How will we reward/recognize employees in the organization?

Team   We will recognize the entire team. Basketball uniforms will be worn for the team picture.

Plug   We will put a plug in for everyone on in-house video. We will plug into a computer network to see what others are doing to recognize their employees. We will encourage people not to chew.

Spin   We will look for as many positive spins as possible within the parameters of credibility. We will make every effort in a crisis to avoid losing our tops.

Pimple   Zit free. We will ensure that recognition will not leave any permanent scars or embarrassments. The focus will be on the positive and not the negative.

Rigid   Advise that there will be times when we must toe the line to meet deadlines but that we will not be rigid all the time. (We will look for opportunities to celebrate "when this phase is over.") Ask the boss to smile.

Art   People will appear in photographs and cartoons and participate in musical jingles and songs. (Art will smile too.)

Reject   When we are brainstorming we will not reject any idea. No one will be a reject. Ideas not selected later will be listed as honorable mention.

Retirement   Is there any way we can continue to recognize retired people who have also contributed? Could we get some bunks in for people who like to take naps? How can we stay hidden during a period when early retirements are being suggested?

Telephone	Get on the phone and tell your boss some of the good things people around you are doing. Obviously, imply that your influence has been positive.
Mountain	Establish goals and graph the upward climb in meeting them. Have a lookout for spotting brush fires.
Sand	Reward people by taking them to the ocean or lake for a picnic. A true grit award may be appropriate.

Here's another example:

Problem: How should we have fun in the office?

Employees	Involve everyone. Don't forget to remember the people who are sick or out on disability.
Knives	How about a Swiss knife for the person who gave us the biggest laugh this month. (Have a "Cut-up" award.)
Story	Prepare a humor history for the firm beginning when the founder of the business (or manager of the bureaucracy) was a baby. Develop legends. Create mythology.
Seal	Get a good housekeeping seal for people who clean up the lunch room. Company event: take disadvantaged children to the zoo to see the monkeys if there are no seals.
Skirt	Ban skirts and suits on a "dress-up" (or dress-down) day. There is no need to skirt the issue.
Man	With the use of a blindfold, pin the nose on a cartoon picture of the face of a grumpy person.
E-mail	Prove your organization has open communications by routing all e-mail to wrong addresses. (Expand this to include the wrong discussion groups on the Internet.)

Candy	Ban the temptation. Create a new place outside the building for candy eaters (next to the smokers).
Rump	Roast someone in good fun on a special occasion. Posters announcing the event could be a real kick.
Instruction	All employees will find something odd about the way the organization does things and something funny about any process or procedure.
Simple	Simple fun. Look at the situation.
Loose	Our thinking will be loose. Any effort to structure and institutionalize ideas for having fun will be run through a paper shredder.

So there you have it. The next time you have a problem pick some random words and see where they lead. If it's both creativity and humor you have a double bonus.

Brainstorming, random words, and off the wall devices are used by advertising agencies. The most creative, the most humorous advertising is what we best remember. We buy the products.

Humor sells—everywhere it goes. (Why should only advertisers know this?)

Chapter Nine

So Then There Was Conflict

Conflict?

Conflict opens doors for humor. Yes it does.

Suppressing conflict can be bad for people and organizations. All out uncontrolled conflict can have the same impact. What is required then is managed conflict, and in this effort, humor is a vehicle.

Common causes of conflict include:

Different Perceptions from Misinformation and Disinformation.

The information may be:

Inaccurate	You told me that the computer was down for three hours.
Outdated	He wears a tie like that?
Contradictory	Last week it was quality. This week it's quality as long as we get it out on time.
Incomplete	It took me a long time to learn this. You can learn it the hard way too.
Misunderstood	I did it just like she told me to do it.
Limited Resources	I'm sure he doesn't mean we need more brains around here.
Competition	For anything and everything. The American way. She gets the promotion. She wins. All the rest of us lose. How do we get even?

There are other causes of conflict as well but this gives the flavor. Even though these seem to be very serious problems, a little situational humor can have an impact in managing and resolving present or potential conflicts. For example, in the promotion problem suggested above, the woman could say when congratulated, "Gee, I don't know what happened. Maybe it's a good time to sell your stock." She laughs at herself and does not play the role of winner at the expense of those around her. She is happy with her achievement but she preserves the relationships with people. You may feel this is unnecessary, if so, there is another way.

How To Succeed with Power

Competition, power, and conflict are all related. But power is where it is in many organizations. It has to be, however, high octane power.

When you hear something is to the fifth power, that means your organization has five levels of management. Only the fifth power has real power. The other four powers will be downloaded if deemed appropriate.

Power to the people is not complete nonsense. For example, when the board of directors of an organization gives the chief executive some discretion this is empowerment at its best.

In an earlier chapter I talked about some things to do to succeed. Now we come to the world of hardball. In a world of power and intense competition you must:

Flatter important people. Do not waste time encouraging unimportant people. The conflict here is that occasionally one of the unimportant becomes successful. Rush in quickly to tell this person you "knew it all the time—that you told your previous boss that you knew he would succeed."

The boss is nearly always right. (Although it may seem impossible, make him look brilliant.) It's not necessary to point out the exception when he is wrong. Write a memo to file pointing out the error and make it available only when the boss is let go. "There is a certain ethical standard that I have for myself even though I know that loyalty is important too." (Something like that is particularly useful when you are asked for your opinion about your previous boss by the big boss.)

Getting credit for other peoples' work is an art form. The conflict arises when someone finds out. If you think there is even a possibility that this could happen be sure to use "we"; for example, "this new idea to improve quality is something we came up with." (In most cases it may not be necessary to suggest who "we" really is. Remember this is a case where the messenger gets the reward.)

Tell people what they want to hear. The messenger is never safe on bad news.

Faint praise for competitors can be helpful, particularly if the peer becomes promoted before you. Faint praise sounds something like this: "Well, given the personal factors that she was faced with, she did quite well don't you think?"

Assess blame for mistakes quietly. It might be good advice to just let it leak out so it appears that you were trying to cover the person for the misdeed. This avoids the blind side "get even" conflict that this person might generate at a later date.

Never openly seek power. This could have the same effect as declaring war. In motivational studies even top executives maintain they are seeking achievement rather than power.

Staying late at night can be profitable. Leave a paper—electronic trail—timing your messages so everyone knows precisely how late you worked.

Determine early the organization's sport. Playing tennis when the in sport is golf can be a career threatening miscalculation

Be on the alert for people who are playing by these same rules and point them out to upper management. This is gutsy and there is no question that it could lead to conflict and hidden agendas, but sometimes desperate actions call for desperate measures. For example, in the sports scenario above say: "Are you aware that X is taking lessons with a golf pro? Wouldn't it be nice if we had his family money?"

So there you are. You can surround yourself with power, avoid roadblocks and unnecessary conflict at the same time. If this seems like too much effort, or simply crass, sit back and laugh at those that do go for it.

Gender Conflict

With the increasing numbers of women in the workplace there are ample opportunities for the genders to misunderstand one another. They do. This has been going on for centuries but sociologists have only recently discovered that the genders do not think alike. (They don't even look alike.)

Today we have hunters and gatherers in the workplace, but we do not know who they are. The roles are changing rapidly and the ensuing events can be funny. For example, when a woman manager asks a male employee: "Will it be possible to have this report done by next week?" he says, "No way." She goes away fuming. By indirection or rhetorical question she wanted the work done next week, but she did not wish to appear bossy. He took it as an inquiry not a request and most certainly not an order.

Generally women think about relationships. Men are "results driven." In the road are a lot of stereotypes. How would you turn these around?

"It is unfeminine for a woman to be aggressive on the job."
(Okay, but where do you want them to be aggressive.)

"The best women managers think like men."
(Can we afford that many mistakes?)

"It is natural for a female present at a meeting to take notes for the group."
(She also knows where to find the cream for the coffee.)

"All men are animals."
(Their mothers saw them as cuddly bears.)

"Men are reluctant to act as mentors for women."
(They get into enough trouble at home as it is.)

Gender-specific words also contribute to the stereotyping problems we have. In figure 9 there are some terms that need correction. We need new, culturally safe terms, to resolve gender-specific words that exist today. (If they have a humorous bent this will reinforce that we can laugh at almost anything.)

Figure 9

Gender Re-Dress

ADVANCE MAN

FOREMAN

CLOTHES MAKE THE MAN

*FALL GUY

DIRTY OLD MAN

FATHER FIGURE

FISHERMAN

GIVE THE DEVIL HIS DUE

GRANDFATHER CLAUSE

LUMBER JACK

MAN ON THE STREET

TRAVELING SALESMAN

YES MAN

LET HER RIP

HANDY MAN

DRAFTSMAN

With words and expressions like this in our language is it surprising that there are conflicts? (For potential answers see Appendix B.)

*I will be changing my name from Fahlman to Fahlperson (or Fahlguy if guy ever becomes politically correct as a genderless term.)

One-Act Plays About Resolving Conflict

The following play demonstrates how conflict works in a win-lose environment:

Same Ol' Same Ol'

Characters:
George: An engineer in Group A
Mary: A supervisor in Group B

Mary: This is a bad time to have a meeting. I had planned a meeting with my people, but, okay, if this is what you want let's go ahead. What's the problem?

George: I have a feeling you are trying to avoid me. We've got to talk about this sometime.

Mary: You engineers are all alike. Everything seems to be at your convenience. Okay, okay, one more time. What's the problem?

George: Your people are not following the specifications I gave them, and as a result, the product has some flaws.

Mary: Who says so?

George: Well...when you get down to it I say so.

Mary: That's odd. We've been putting this product out a long time, and this is the first time I've heard about it.

George: I talked to my boss about it, and he said he talked to your boss.

Mary: My boss often talks to me about the quantity and quality of work, but he never mentioned that your boss had talked to him.

George: Well, he did.

Mary: Why didn't you come talk to me about it?

George: You're never available.

Mary: That's not true.

George: If I didn't become obnoxious we wouldn't even have this meeting.

Mary: You know my boss has said we're doing a great job on our product. The quality is there and we're getting it out on time.

George: Your boss is not a bad guy, but I don't think he knows just how important it is to have zero defects.

Mary: Zero defects are wonderful if you have unlimited dollars. If we did everything your way we would have only one product to sell, but it would be perfect.

George: That's fuzzy and unprofessional thinking. You women are all emotional.

Mary: You're deliberately trying to make me mad.

George: No, I'm not. I'm really restraining myself. But what you are doing is making our product look bad, and of course the customers tell our sales representatives that it is poor engineering.

Mary: Sounds to me like you don't have the entire picture.

George: Well, you certainly don't or at least some of your people don't.

Mary: I see no reason to continue this discussion. I can't see us agreeing on anything.

George: If you just approached this logically. Well, it looks to me like the next meeting will have to be with your department head.

So there you have it—a real conflict. Neither is worrying about solving the problem or preserving the relationship. Imagine that *Mary* and *George* are both seven years old at a playground and listen again to their conversation. It's funny.

One can't help wondering how humor might have helped resolve this problem. Suppose George had started this way:

"Hi Mary. I need your help. As you probably know we in engineering think the axis of the world goes right through our department, and (smiling) of course there is a measure of truth to that. And we see flaws. As a matter of fact we couldn't get a degree in engineering without demonstrating the ability to assess blame. But I'm not here to do that today. Our customers say we have a product problem, and I need your help in determining what we should do about it."

Do you think if George had laughed at himself here that resolution might have been possible? How conflicts originate is a mystery. Watching them develop is frustrating, but with a little perspective, very funny. Watch how this group handles interaction in the play called:

"The Packets"

Cast:
Mark: Sales
Engie: Engineer
Arn: Production

Mark: I'm glad we could get together. I've got a major problem to talk to you about.

Engie: It's not those customized customer packets again is it?

Arn: Well, if it is, then it's going to cost us some money.

Mark: What's going to cost us money?

Engie: Hope this meeting doesn't take too long. I've got some real work to do.

Arn: Having customized customer packets is going to cause us a lot of extra work. Frankly, I don't think we have the people to do it, and I strongly believe we should hire some additional people right now.

Mark: Oh come on. You're an alarmist. We can get it done with the existing work force. Cost us a little overtime, that's all. Ajax Electronics does want a customized packet to accompany each unit. It is for their employees so that they will have clear instructions in how to use what we send them. The units we're sending are unique, and they think that we should supply customer information to match. It seems like a reasonable request to me.

Arn: Do you think the customer would be willing to pay for it?

Mark: *(Shrugs without answering)*

Engie: That makes sense to me but I don't think it's going to cost much money.

Arn: How can you say that?

Engie: What has to be done that is so radically different? I do, however, oppose it on principle. We've put this product out for over twenty customers, and we have never had to come up with a separate instruction book for anyone. Why Ajax?

Mark: They've asked for it. That's why. There is a lot of potential at Ajax and if we want repeat business…

Engie: *(Interrupting)* You sales types are all alike. All you want is to make sales.

Mark: Now that isn't true…I am worried about customer service and I think…

Arn: *(Interrupting)* Look, if we make this change it will not only cost us a lot of money, but we can't be sure that we will be able to maintain the same quality that we have now.

Mark: Okay. You guys go talk to the customer if you don't believe me. Now listen. I think we're blowing this thing way out of perspective. We're not talking about many modifications. I may have to go to my vice-president on this if we can't resolve it.

Arn: I'm going to my vice-president too, because this is going to cost us money.

Engie: I'm understaffed as well. I have no one that I can release to do this *(said slowly, sarcastically)* CUSTOM job.

Mark: You don't have to be sarcastic.

Engie: I wasn't sarcastic, just being factual.

Mark: Thanks anyway, folks. One more time...you'll do it your way. Someday when you're all laid off because we don't have any customers...

Arn: *(Interrupting)* That's a bit melodramatic.

Engie: Tell me again. What are we suppose to be doing here?

This group is a long way from conflict resolution. Unfortunately it sounds like many meetings in organizations. If they were children all participants would have time-outs in a corner. As a spectator, however, humor abounds.

Aikido Humor

Aikido is an ancient martial art where the prime principle is to "go with the flow." At the risk of simplification, it means that rather than using energy to deflect the blow or counterattack, you move with the thrust in the same direction or slightly altered direction.

The same applies to aikido humor. You go with the flow. This is particularly useful when an angry, irrational, or emotional thrust is directed at you personally. Humor doesn't come easily at this juncture so you agree, or appear to agree, with the attacker in a humorous way. In actual problem solving you might say something that goes with the flow but is followed by a response such as: "Okay, now what can we do to help improve this situation, solve the problem, make it right, etc."

Here's an example. If someone says: "You're the slowest person I've ever dealt with," your aikido response might be: "But I was selected home-room president." The person making the attack has, at the very least, to shake his head.

Here is another real life situation offered by workshop participant Rashelle Turner.

A worker was taking verbal abuse from a customer.

"What happened to my appointment, stupid?"

The worker apologized, indicating that the delay was unavoidable.

"Who's running this place, stupid?"

The worker responded.

After the response the unhappy customer asked, "What's your name?"

To which the employee responded, "I guess it has to be Stupid," much to the delight of other customers waiting in line.

Aikido humor is a release valve that makes it possible to bring things back to a normal situation. (You still want to solve the problem, but you do not want, or need, to be attacked.)

In Figure 10 there are several statements you might encounter at work which merit an aikido response. Remember, the secret is to go with the flow (perhaps even through feigned misunderstanding) and not to be defensive or fight back.

Figure 10

Aikido Statements

YOUR HAIR IS TOO LONG.

CAN'T YOU MOVE A LITTLE FASTER?

ARE YOU SERIOUS?

ARE YOU KIDDING?

THEY'LL NEVER BUY THAT.

YOUR SKIRT IS TOO SHORT.

WHY DIDN'T YOU THINK ABOUT THIS BEFORE YOU DID IT?

DON'T YOU UNDERSTAND PLAIN ENGLISH?

DIDN'T YOU TAKE THE MESSAGE?

HOW MANY TIMES HAVE I TOLD YOU TO SAVE WHAT YOU'VE WRITTEN ON THE COMPUTER?

(POWER AT THE COPY MACHINE): HOW LONG WILL YOU BE?

NICE GOING. THIS CUSTOMER IS GOING TO BE MAD.

IN THE OLD DAYS PEOPLE WORKED.

IT HAPPENED ON YOUR SHIFT.

WHY CAN'T YOU BE LOGICAL?

YOU'RE NOT SUGGESTING WE DO THAT ARE YOU?

There are some potential responses in Appendix B.

There will be times when you cannot come up with any quick one-liners to match the rude, aggressive or unacceptable statements directed at you personally.

Here are some good all purpose, "clueless" answers to have ready:

"I'M SORRY, WE DON'T HAVE A PUBLIC REST ROOM."

"HOW DID YOU KNOW I WAS THE FIRST BORN IN MY FAMILY?"

"I'VE BEEN ADOPTED TWICE."

"I GOT THE JOB BECAUSE OF SUPERIOR GENES. MY DAD. HE OWNS THE STORE."

"I HAD SOME RELATIVES IN MONTANA TOO."

"COULD YOU WHISPER. I HAVE A HEARING PROBLEM."

"MAYBE I DID. SOME SAY I WAS A GIRAFFE IN A PREVIOUS LIFE."

"YES, I DO HAVE A TOUCH OF DIARRHEA."

Stereotypes

Stereotypes have great humor potential.

Here are some common (mis) beliefs about human behavior with some aside comment. (You can add your own.)

RED-HAIRED PEOPLE ARE MORE QUICK TEMPERED THAN BLONDES OR BRUNETTES. (DOES THIS MEAN THAT THEY NO LONGER HAVE A BAD TEMPER WHEN THEY BECOME GRAY?)

SLOW LEARNERS REMEMBER MORE THAN FAST LEARNERS. (THEY PROBABLY SHOULD TALK FASTER TO MAKE UP FOR IT.)

GENIUS IS CLOSE TO INSANITY. (THEY'VE BEEN KNOWN TO SIT NEXT TO EACH OTHER IN A BAR.)

HIGH PERFORMING EMPLOYEES ALWAYS MAKE THE BEST MANAGERS. (IF NOTHING ELSE, THEY WILL ALWAYS BE AROUND TO SHOW THE TROOPS THE "RIGHT WAY TO DO THINGS.")

NICE GUYS FINISH LAST. (IS IT ALSO TRUE THAT GOOD GIRLS DON'T GO INTO LOCKER ROOMS?)

True Conflict Resolution

There is hope for all of us in resolving conflict. Pat Ross shares with us a recent flare-up with the fire department.

Ms. Ross
61 SW Minnehaha
Lake Oswego, OR

Dear Ms. Ross,

Our office has received complaints about the tall grass in your yard. Once these weeds start to dry up, they will become a fire hazard and a danger to your property and your neighbors.

At this time, we are asking you to cut and remove the tall weeds. Once it becomes a fire hazard, it may be referred to Clackamas County District Attorney for possible prosecution. Our office would appreciate you removing the weeds before it becomes a problem.

If our office can help, please feel free to call us.

Sincerely,

John McCauley
Fire Marshal

Mom Ross' U-Pick Weed A Rama

Fire Marshal
City of Lake Oswego
351 SW 1st
Lake Oswego, OR 97034

Dear F. Marshal:

Received your epistle yesterday re: the tall weeds in my yard. You indicated these could become a fire hazard when they "dry out." Really now, can we talk? This is western Oregon—home of the banana slug with three days of sunshine guaranteed annually. Chances are these weeds will never "dry out." In fact, I performed a little experiment on them and determined the fastest way to dry them is to apply gasoline followed by a flick of the Bic. This doesn't smell very nice, though, and tends to make the lawn look like asphalt.

What we're talking here is not a fire hazard; it's your basic visual pollution from the eyes of some beholders. You probably won't be a bit interested to learn that I've applied for protected status as a Horticultural Refuse Area. Unfortunately, even my registration as a Republican is cutting no weight with the current administration. My poor weeds are becoming endangered.

You and the other clipped lawn connoisseurs will probably rejoice that many of the little darlings have been plucked from the front yard already and a yard service hired to deal with the rest.

Sincerely,

Occupant

61 SW Minnehaha
Lake Oswego, OR

Dear Ms. Occupant

I thank you so much for your cooperation in correcting the weed complaint.

I am very flattered as I have never had my feeble attempts at letter writing considered formal or elegant. You have made my day.

We of the Fire Department would hope that you do not use gasoline as a form of land clearing, besides, DEQ would undoubtedly be upset with that approach.

Within the physical boundaries of the city, a horticultural permit of the nature you were proposing would not be approved. However, you are in the county and they may not view the problem the same way city planners might.

Needless to say, I enjoyed your letter very much because most letters that I received are not humorous or friendly. If you are not writing professionally you are wasting your talents.

Thank you again for making your weeds an endangered species.

Sincerely

John McCauley, Fire Marshal

As you can see, conflict resolution is possible by lighting up. (Or is it lighten?)

Chapter Ten

Humor That Should Not Be

Is it strange that I should talk about humor and then suggest some of it might not be appropriate? Absolutely not. Bad humor does more harm than no humor at all.

There are the obvious kinds of humor that do not belong in the work place (or anywhere in our opinion). These include dirty jokes, ethnic or crass humor.

We say that these efforts at humor ought to be avoided at all costs. Why? Because they—particularly ethnic and off color jokes—provide the opportunity to hurt feelings, cause resentment and anger as well as close the doors for creativity, openness, and trust.

Have you ever known someone who in your presence disparaged every possible group and most of the people they knew? How did you feel? That you might be next in a session you weren't attending? The same applies to humor. If someone can tell those jokes on "them," then they can do the same for me or "us." In the humanity of men\women if "they" are "stupid" and butts of jokes, then so are we.

Time for realism. This lower reaches humor exists. We just suggest that it is an important judgment call—particularly at work. "I was only kidding" is one test that you can apply. If you must use this expression, then most likely, the humor wasn't appropriate in the first place.

Different materials which have circulated around organizations such as "Sexual Harassment Will Not be Reported but it will be Graded," may be funny in some circles, but it is not funny to someone who has experienced sexual harassment.

Following are other examples:

The Rules:

> The female always makes the rules
>
> The rules are subject to change at any time without prior notification.
>
> The female has the right to be upset or angry at any time
>
> The male must remain calm at all times, unless the female wants him to be angry or upset.

and/or

Seminars for Men:

> Reasons to Give Flowers
>
> Filling Ice Trays
>
> How to Go Shopping with Your Mate Without Getting Lost

How to Put the Toilet Seat Down

How to Overcome Dependency to the Remote Control

In the right circles this humor may be acceptable. If you have any doubts at all don't take the chance.

Sarcasm and Satire

Any sarcasm directed at someone as a personal attack is clearly not acceptable.

Any sarcasm, satire, or irony directed toward our old favorite "company policy" or tension or stress or anything (ridiculous) generated by "staff" or "headquarters" is absolutely acceptable. Of course some senior managers will tell you differently.

These same managers would look askance at all those little messages posted around our desks. But these notes permit us to retain our sanity.

Here are some favorites:

"OH DONKEY POOP! YOU DID IT JUST THE WAY I TOLD YOU."

"FRANKLY YOUR BUSINESS MEANS NOTHING TO US...OTHER THAN CLOTHING, FOOD, AND SHELTER"

"THIS JOB ATE MY BRAIN."

"SINCE THEY DON'T PAY ME TO THINK DO I REALLY NEED A BRAIN?"

"THIS TOO SHALL PASS."

"I'VE GOT ONE NERVE LEFT. HOW DID YOU FIND IT?"

"YOU WANT IT WHEN?"

"YESTERDAY'S A MEMORY. TOMORROW'S A DREAM. TODAY'S A PAIN IN THE BUTT."

"HUMOR. NEVER LEAVE HOME WITHOUT IT."

"Due to Budget Constraints the Light at the End of the Tunnel Will be Turned Off until Further Notice."

"No Snivelers."

"Are You Lonely. Hold a Meeting."

"We Cannot Continue to do More and More with Less and Less."

"Of All the Things I've Lost I Miss My Mind the Most."

Every once in a while a classic memo is written that reaches us all. The following satirical, hilarious memo reappears somewhere in the bureaucratic world every eight minutes.

TO: All Employees

SUBJECT: New Rest Room Procedure

In the past, employees were permitted to make trips to the rest rooms under informal guidelines. Effective the beginning of next month, a Rest Room Trip Policy (RTP) will be established to provide a consistent method of accounting for each employee's rest room times and ensuring equal treatment of all employees.

Under this policy, a "REST ROOM TRIP BANK" (RTB) will be established for each employee. The first day of each month, employees will be given a REST ROOM TRIP CREDIT (RTC) of twenty. Rest room credits can be accumulated from month to month.

Starting next month, the entrance to all rest rooms will be equipped with personnel identification stations and computer-linked voice print recognition devices. Before the end of this month, each employee must provide two copies of voice prints (one normal, one under stress) to the System Operator. The voice print recognition stations will be operational but not restrictive, for the first month; employees should acquaint themselves with the stations during that period.

If an employee's REST ROOM TRIP BANK balance reaches zero, the doors of the rest room will not unlock for the employee's voice until the first of the next month. In addition, all rest room stalls are being equipped with timed paper roll retractors. If the stall is occupied for more than three minutes, an alarm will sound. Thirty seconds after the alarm sounds, the roll of paper in the stall will retract, the toilet will flush and the stall door will open. If the stall remains occupied, your picture will be taken.

The picture will then be posted on the bulletin board located outside the cafeteria. This is being done to eliminate "dilly-dallying" in the rest rooms. Anyone whose picture shows up three times will immediately be terminated.

One final caution: this system will always work if you go to the rest room where you have been assigned. We cannot guarantee that your voice print will work in other rest rooms in the building, and we suggest you not test it—particularly if the urge is pressing.

If you have any questions about the new policy, please ask your supervisor.

There are some who think that this widely circulated memo is totally unacceptable. Why? It could be that it sounds too authentic. When this has been read in jest to some work groups, there are some people who really believe it. After all, "It sounds a lot like the other memos we get around here."

Joke-Joke

The greatest laughter in organizations doesn't come from joke-jokes. These are jokes with a beginning, a middle, and a punch line. They are contrived, of course, "to get a laugh." Many do. Stand-up comics work hard to develop this form of humor and many are successful.

They cannot, however, compare to situational humor—to a humor that comes about spontaneously. We can all think of comedians who brought down the house with situational humor—talking about everyday life and current news and happenings. Of course they have an arsenal of jokes, but they have learned to adapt them to current situations.

Think of the latest explosion of laughter in your work group. It may have been an urgency breaker situation that created the humor. If you were to repeat what happened to someone who wasn't there, it may not seem quite as funny. You know, however, it was funny and good for the group.

Eliminating joke-jokes in the workplace (or anyplace else) is a lost cause. All I am suggesting is that there is something better.

Gallows Humor

Another kind of humor that is finding its way into many work groups today is something called gallows humor. It is usually so grim that one has to ask if it is humor at all. The problem is that many managements are acting in such a manner that promotes this kind of humor.

I am reminded of the cartoonist pictorial of a stork trying to swallow the frog and the frog is grabbing the stork by the throat before he goes down the throat. The caption reads: "Don't Ever Give Up." Most of us would agree that this isn't the funniest cartoon we've ever heard about. It is, unfortunately, a statement of truth in many organizations where restructuring, downsizing, and indiscriminate layoffs has taken precedence over people. The stress caused by these actions then finds its way into grim humor.

If you have a lot of the "humor" displayed in Figure 11 then your organization has a long way to go before it can re-capture real humor (and real employee commitment).

Figure 11 (Company name withheld to prevent sharp reactions on Wall Street)

EMPLOYEE SALE

That's right friends...You heard it here first

It will cost us too much to lay them off

SO WE'RE SELLING THEM

We must get down to our new one employee

per business unit goal, and you can help us

All races, creeds, colors, religions,

sexes and sexual orientations available

YOU SAY YOU WANT NEW

We've got 'em

Employees with Low Mileage

High performance and a lot of years left

YOU SAY YOU WANT OLD RELIABLES

We've Got 'em—The paint's a little gray and

They grumble a little but they've seen it all

And keep on working

We've been laying them off for years and losing

All that severance pay

Now you can help us make

A Little Money in the Process

SO...COME ONE, COME ALL TO THE FIRST

ANNUAL EMPLOYEE SALE

(Buy two and get a free VCR)

Chapter Eleven

Formulas That Work

Throughout this primer you have seen some devices that help you see the humor around you—your own humor and that which exists in your organization. There are additional formulas that will guide you to even greater fun.

Admit it. Where you work there are a few things that are boring, trivial, or routine. There are also things that are stressful, agonizing, and disturbing.

They must not take over your existence, creating negative energy. So here is the first formula: No matter how disgusting, boring, or stressful some person or activity may be, it is your job to find "the very good thing about" (it).

Here's an example:

"The very good thing about your competition is that it is a place where you can send your disagreeable customers."

Here is another possibility:

"The very good thing about junk mail is that you get to read the mail of someone called Car RT SORT."

You can look at these and more in Figure 12.

Figure 12

The Very Good Thing About...

Junk Mail

Competitors

Company Policies

Puddles

E-Mail

New Programs

Giraffes

Instructions for VCRs and Computer Programs

Bosses

Public Affairs

People in the Plant

People in the Office

The year 2008

Laptop Computers

JOINT VENTURES

TENSION

STRESS

STIFF JOINTS

STUDENTS

FOREPERSONS

SUPERVISORS

NEW EMPLOYEES

CORPORATE CULTURES

CONSULTANTS

MAINFRAMES

INTERNET

PANIC

URGENCY

STUPID QUESTIONS

GLASS CEILINGS

TANGENTS

BEING ABSENT MINDED

WEAK BLADDERS

(See Appendix B for answers.)

Remember, the "very good thing about" is a useful tool for all occasions, but it's particularly valuable in the case of bad news. Even with something bad there is something good. For example: "We don't have to worry about the bad news anymore. It has already happened."

The Answer Person

This formula made popular by Steve Allen has been used by other entertainers. We've come up with answers. All you need to do is think of questions that might fit the bill.

Here is an example:

They don't like change. The question might be: "Why do people like dollar bills?" or "Why don't babies cry more often?"

There are more answers in Figure 13. Your job is to supply the questions.

Figure 13

JUST DO IT

HEMLINES ARE CHANGING

DISPOSABLE DIAPERS

BUDGET DEFICIT

LIMIT BOOKS TO TEN CHAPTERS

TO AVOID HANG UPS

HANGOVERS

THAT'S HOW THE COOKIE CRUMBLES

JUST IN TIME

WE'RE ON A ROLL

(See Appendix B)

Buzz Words and Clichés

There are an incredulous number of clichés in the organization world. Those that follow will be completely forgotten by the year 2005.

Since there may be people who do not know the significance of these clichés, help them. Record whatever comes to your mind when you see them. That's the name of this game. Again, you will be doing new people in your organization a great service by telling them what they mean (or could mean).

Figure 14

STATE OF THE ART

PRO-ACTIVE

LEVEL PLAYING FIELD

MOMMY TRACK

QUALITY CIRCLES

WHAT GOES AROUND COMES AROUND

THE WHOLE NINE YARDS

WORST CASE SCENARIO

ZERO DEFECT

SLIDING SCALE

CO-DEPENDENT

BRAINSTORM

BURN-OUT

TIME MANAGEMENT

BACK TO BASICS

IF YOUR CUP RUNNETH OVER

(See Appendix B)

Definitions

Cousin to clichés are many words that simply need more specific definitions, particularly in the organization world. Your job is to come up with a definition that could make sense (or nonsense):

Figure 15

FAX

BIG BLUE

GM

DOWNSCALING

RE-ENGINEERING

PC

OVERHEAD

DESKTOP

CRITICAL PATH

The computer field is one area that defies clear understanding of the vocabulary. Help those around you by giving meaningful definitions for the following:

RAM

ROM

ORPHANS

FULL MOUSE SUPPORT

POP-UP UTILITIES

ON LINE

SPREADSHEET

SHARED INTERFACE

MULTI-BOOT

WINDOWS

USER FRIENDLY

You can find some other answers in Appendix B.

Tom Swifties in the Workplace

Here is another formula for generating humor. I could live for ever on Tom Swifties (from the old children's books of the same name), but if I did I would quickly lose family, friends, and co-workers. For this reason we suggest you introduce Swifties gradually. Here is how it works. Use adverbs with the suffix "ly" giving a slightly different meaning for the general thought being presented.

Note these examples:

"The print is dark," he said _____.

You might suggest: "This print is dark," he said boldly.

"She stole my wallet and pants," the victim said _____.

Here is a possibility: "She stole my wallet and pants," the victim said briefly.

Here are some workplace opportunities to speed you on:

"I'm glad that the copy machine is working again," she said _____.

"Indiscriminate drilling for oil can be disastrous," the environmentalist said _____.

"The full disclosure of information is imperfect in this case," the attorney said _____.

"Employees who do not work should be released," the supervisor said _____.

"This patient has made little progress," the nurse said _____.

"She is a welcome addition to the office but not for the reason you're thinking," the manager said _____.

"You just can't buy loyalty any more," the union negotiator said _____.

"Giving the shirt off your back can lead to other problems," the non-giver said _____, "particularly if it's a blouse," she said _____.

"Our departments don't see eye to eye on anything," the director said _____.

"Many persons come to work in a variety of shoe wear," the supervisor observed _____.

"I will not do it the way the boss wants me to," the employee said _____.

"The mommy track is a concept that should be rejected _____," said the vice-president of personnel.

"Many job re-classifications will be redone," said the Human Resources manager _____.

"I have no idea how the theft took place," the security guard said _____.

"All criminals will probably find their way to hell," the warden said _____.

"I think I'll take this to a higher court," the attorney said _____.

"There is no excuse for writing like that," the author said _____.

"When I'm away from work I feel guilty," the worker said _____.

"I am not sure that Maslow's theory applies," the psychologist said _____.

"You say the computer has a virus," the operator asked _____.

"I would just as soon not have anyone know about this computer problem," she said _____.

"The boss has a boiling point," the secretary said _____.

"If I were you I wouldn't let that get out," the security person said _____.

"Don't worry about these bonds falling," the broker said _____.

"I have an opinion on that," the newscaster said _____.

"I think we should follow the letter of the law," the judge said _____.

"I question that the bridge will hold up," the engineer said_____

"We have much too much scrap," the supervisor said _____.

"We must get guns off the street," the police chief said _____.

"I hate to part with this desk," the executive said _____.

"Can we find out who wrote this?" the editor asked _____.

"Where were you when the earthquake began?" the seismologist asked _____.

"A portion of the cemetery will have to be sold to the city," the planner said _____.

"Getting a big bonus is as easy as leading lambs to slaughter," the CEO said _____.

Undoubtedly you have come up with a few "groaners" that will work well in the office. See appendix B for answers.

Matching Phrases For Organizations

Another useful activity is matching two lists of phrases—another good warm-up for getting a group to work together. Match the best alphabetical listing with the most appropriate number.

A. WHAT IS A SWINGING SINGLE?

B. HE INSISTED HE WAS A MONKEY'S UNCLE.

C. THE HATCHET JOB WAS ELIMINATED.

D. CAN I GET INTO THE BUREAU?

E. SAVE, SAVE, SAVE.

F. THE SUITS CONTROL EVERYTHING.

G. "IT'S VERY STUFFY IN HERE," SHE SAID.

H. THEY PUT A NEW SPIN ON THINGS.

I. SHE WAS LAST SEEN IN THE ACCOUNTING DEPARTMENT.

J. WHAT DOES A NUDIST BEACH DO FOR THE ECONOMY?

K. SEX AND THE OFFICE DON'T MIX.

L. WHY DON'T YOU LIKE MIDDLE MANAGEMENT?

M. WOULD YOU ADDRESS YOUR INTENTIONS?

Now match each of these with one of the possibilities below:

1. AND HE TOOK A CUT IN SALARY.

2. NOTHING BUT WHO CARES?

3. BECAUSE THAT'S WHERE I PUT ON WEIGHT.

4. SOMEONE WHO DOESN'T BUNT.

5. ISN'T NEPOTISM A SHAME?

6. FORTUNATELY THE BOSS HAD A HEARING LOSS.

7. THE COMPUTER BURPED.

8. SHE WAS NEITHER A CREDIT NOR DEBIT TO THE FIRM.

9. YET THEY ARE OFTEN CAUGHT WITH THEIR PANTS DOWN.

10. BUT THE CHAIRS STILL NEEDED OIL.

11. PEOPLE WASTE ENOUGH TIME AS IT IS.

12. SURE, BUT THEY CLOSE THE DRAWERS EVERY NIGHT.

13. IF YOU GIVE ME THE ZIP CODE.

Okay, had enough? All right then, finish the alphabet.

More Matches

N. THE ENGINEERS AND PRODUCTION PEOPLE HAVE FINALLY REACHED AN AGREEMENT.

O. HOW CAN WE CUT OUR TAXES?

P. HOW DO YOU KNOW TO PROCEED WITH CAUTION?

Q. HE IS LIKE A COMPUTER NETWORK.

R. HIS DOOR IS ALWAYS OPEN.

S. WHERE DID THEY GET THIS NEW CHARACTER?

T. SHE DRESSES FOR SUCCESS.

U. WE SAW YOU ON THE MONITOR.

V. THEY WANTED FULL DISCLOSURE.

W. HE TAKES A NAP IN THE AFTERNOON

X. THE SALESPERSON OFTEN OVERSOLD CUSTOMERS.

Y. WHY DO WE WORK SO MUCH OVERTIME?

Z. SHE MADE A LOT OF DOUGH FOR THE COMPANY.

Match with the phrases below:

14. HE'S RETIRED ON THE JOB.

15. SHE SEPARATES THE WHEAT FROM THE CHAFF.

16. TAKE A REDUCTION IN PAY.

17. WE'RE INTERESTED IN YOUR SECURITY.

18. HE GIVES US AN ON-LINE HEADACHE.

19. ONLY HIS MIND IS CLOSED.

20. HE MADE THE PRESIDENT'S CLUB AGAIN THIS YEAR.

21. WHEN BOTH THE AUDITOR AND THE IRS INQUIRE ABOUT BUSINESS MEALS.

22. HE CAME WITH CHAPTER 11.

23. SHE RELUCTANTLY LET THEM LOOK AT HER BRIEFS.

24. SHE GETS EXPOSURE WITHOUT EXPOSURE.

25. THEY NO LONGER TALK TO EACH OTHER AT ALL.

26. THE CLOCKS MOVE FASTER THAN THE PEOPLE.

Having made the matches it is obvious that they need work. Your creativity and humor require more. Therefore take the opportunity now to come up with new matching phrases in the number column.

Finally, rediscover the old proverbs of the last two centuries and see where they might fit into your organization.

Proverbs

Figure 1

A bad workman quarrels with his tools. (And his boss, his peers, his customers, his spouse, and with TV commentators.)

To put one's best foot forward. (Keep it out of your mouth.)

Birds of a feather flock together. (The commute will not be easy again today.)

To blow one's own trumpet. (But tell your boss she inspired your playing in tune.)

The day is short and work is long. (Overtime pay is only possible for hourly workers.)

To have a finger in the pie. (We will pass up the next potluck.)

To know which way the wind blows. (Stand pat. Management will change their mind several times.)

Mind your own business. (The state and federal government will help you.)

There is a screw loose somewhere. (Do you have nepotism in your organization?)

To split hairs. (This is a good idea for older workers who are balding.)

You cannot see the woods for the trees. (Have you ever seen a clear-cut forest?)

To make a clean breast of it. (This is highly unusual wording; it means truth in packaging.)

You've done it! No more formulas. Remember, though, one can get a lot of humor mileage out of "the very good thing about," clichés, definitions, answers, matching phrases, and proverbs.

Perspective

Here's another memo, this time from the manager of a regional subsidiary to the parent organization.

To: Jeffrey Williams, President, Amalgamated

Subject: Manifestly Unimportant Numbers

It is getting toward the end of the year and a summary of what is happening here in our organization is appropriate. We had high hopes that some of the things we've been working on would straighten themselves out but it doesn't look as if that will be the case.

First it appears that the business may lose its favorable bond rating. Our Comptroller left the organization for the Canary Islands, and we are missing substantial amounts of money in bonds and equities.

It further appears that our plan of giving money to selected politicians is illegal, and the local press has managed to find out about it.

Apparently one of our divisions has dumped considerable amounts of waste products in ten different rivers, and the Department of Environmental Quality and Department of Justice will make a joint announcement on the penalty very shortly.

Our engineering department is now talking to representatives of the EEOC in an effort to avoid charges of discrimination.

You may remember Annabell Jones. (How could you forget Annabell Jones?) She has filed a sexual harassment suit against two of our middle managers.

We, of course, have faced adversities before, but we believe that we will overcome these and drive on to bigger and better things in the year to come.

Sincerely,

Alex DuBest, Manager

Nu-Sight Enterprises

P.S. Before you have a seizure I want you to know that none of the above has happened. What has happened is that our sales are 10 percent below objective, and we wanted you to realize that, in view of what could have happened, these numbers are manifestly unimportant.

Who knows. It might work. Certainly it's another perspective.

In the vignette that follows workshop participant Carol L. Doane puts in perspective many of the things we have discussed here:

The time I laughed so hard no sound came out was back in the spring of 1982. I was green, wet behind the ears, and unsure of myself in a new sales position at a Pacific Northwest newspaper. Due to a tad bit of insecurity and being a little high strung, I was acutely aware of my surroundings at all times. The veteran on our staff, well past his prime, prone to slapping rulers on desks to punctuate a long forgotten point in one of many long tirades on selling in the good old days, strolled across the sales floor.

Usually I meant to avoid him, so my subconscious registered the movement and quickly scanned for escape routes. The direction he had come from abruptly reached a conscious level as I caught a glimpse of a long white tail of toilet paper trailing from his pants all the way down his backside. Yes, I had heard of this happening before, but had never experienced it as participant or spectator.

I began gesturing wildly, somewhat convulsively, to a male staff member, hoping desperately he would jump in and save the old guy from total, annihilating embarrassment. He did save the day, and very graciously escorted him off the sales floor. This could be a good example of something funny happening in the workplace. It could also be an opportunity to make fun, tease or trivialize a co-worker, an unhealthy work habit to adopt.

Let's look at another event. After years of conflict between the outside and inside sales force, emotions hit a crisis point one snowy day in the middle of a cold winter. The manager gathered the mixed sales force in a small, heavily windowed conference room The discussion heated up the room like no climate control thus known.

Passions boiled over when an inside rep accused outside reps of doing their Christmas shopping on company time.

The room grew silent after several sharp intakes of breath. Outside salespeople unleashed their sales claws while sales fangs bared themselves behind nervous quivering lips. This was a room of sales animals ready to pounce with sales adrenaline running on high, primed for a kill. The manager in charge of the meeting teetered on the knife's edge of an ugly explosion of defensive anger, a possible homicide, and her managerial concern to keep the room under control. Fine, upstanding career professionals had been accused of the worst transgression known to their trade, i.e. squandering precious sales time on selfish acts of shopping. The outside reps meant to set the record straight at any expense.

Unknown to many in the room, behind the cool professional and pristine demeanor of their manager, lurked a prankster somewhere near the level of a sorority sister. In unladylike fashion the manager led the call to arms with the charge, "Take her outside and pants her!" The room erupted with laughter as each person looked outside at the heavy dusting of snow and imagined the well-deserved feel of ice on a bare butt. Sure, some left the room in a huff, some just shaking their heads, and one or two making a note to themselves to be more careful next Christmas. But with a little humor the manager expressed how seriously she took the accusation, not very, and she diffused the highly charged anger that threatened the good work she was trying to accomplish by combining the staff.

A busy day in another newspaper, found the very competent receptionist suddenly inundated with phone calls. She deftly put each caller on hold and then started with the first working her way to the last, by saying, 'Thank you for holding may I help you? Thank you for holding may I help you? Thank you for holding may I help you? Thank you for helping may I hold you? Oops."

So, what does the toilet paper tail, pantsing the inside sales rep, and holding helpful callers have to do with a better workplace? If we look at it with any eye for merriment, it's quite simple, it releases tension. When we can laugh at ourselves, no matter how embarrassing or silly, it gives us all a gentle jolt of humor that makes the day just a little brighter and, in some cases, a little more tolerable. It tells us not to take ourselves so seriously, to enjoy life, enjoy work, and appreciate the people around us more.

One more time: It's worth the quest. For better communication. For better health. For resolution of conflict. For creative stimulation. For reduction of stress and peace of mind. For a better perspective. And finally for people connection.

Laughing nine to five—humor in the workplace—is where it is.

Appendix A

Memos From Management

Memo Subject: Weight Control

In monitoring our health costs we have reviewed the health records of our employees furnished by our managed health-care coordinator.

We are deeply disturbed to find that 40 percent of our employees are overweight. Of course this could lead to even more costly health problems for the corporation.

One of the steps we plan to implement is to limit overweight people's access to elevators. An electronic card will be issued to all employees which will reveal the recommended weight for their height and weight. Upon entering an elevator an electronic eye will scan your body and determine whether you exceed the recommended weight. If you do an alarm will go off.

A recorded voice will then advise you to walk up the stairs to your destination point.

If you forget to wear your card or attempt to foil the electronic system in other ways the elevator door will not close, the alarm will intensify in decibels, and security people will be sent to help you out of the elevator.

This is the first in a number of preventive medicine measures we plan to take to reduce our health costs.

Memo Subject: New Badges

People are our most important asset. To ensure that we keep this in mind, we are issuing badges so that we can keep track of everyone's identity.

Each person will have a badge with a recent picture and social security number on it. If a person does not wear a badge, he/she cannot expect to have the same privileged treatment of other employees. Without the badge one could be treated like a corporate spy, supplier, or customer.

Please wear your badge at all times. Don't be concerned about the inferred dehumanizing of the number on your badge. It is only there as an emergency measure. Only if we can no longer determine who you are by your picture, will we identify you by your number.

Memo Subject: New Telephone Technology

In an effort to cut down on social and family calls, new memory has been introduced in our telephone system to terminate telephone conversations when company business is not being conducted.

The identification of the words that will trigger the implementation of this device is highly confidential, but certain phraseology such as "What did you tell your wife?" and "Don't hit your sister" are sure ways of triggering the device.

It is extremely important to be articulate in your speech. There may be times when your conversation is cut off in error. For example, there may be difficulty with the words "lighting" and "fighting." Certainly "techs" and "sex" are not the same, but with poor articulation, both could result in cutoff conversations (and other problems).

We recognize there may be some bugs in the system, but some are intended.

Memo Subject: School Closure for Inclement Weather and Other Acts of Higher Authority

It is important to understand how to cope with Acts of Nature. There are many potential alternatives available to the people in higher authority at the college:

There may be full closure.

There may be a morning-only closure.

There may be a delay in opening (partial closure).

There may be an evening closure.

There may be an emergency closure.

For a special one-time only event there may be no closure.

To get closure on closure call the college switchboard. If it is jammed accept this as evidence that the deans (re: higher authority cited above) are considering closure.

Memo Subject: Total Quality Management

Your dedication to Total Quality Management has exceeded all of our expectations. There has been continuous improvement, not only of our product, but the processes involved in making it. This, we feel certain, is due to your rigid and enthusiastic adherence to the principles of TQM.

This is true in all facets of our operation. For example, in statistical control we see less than one defect per thousand. As a result we will no longer require final quality checks by quality inspectors.

We would like you to keep up the good work wherever you may be employed in the future. For reasons other than quality, we're sure, we are no longer able to sell our typewriters.

Memo Subject: Dress Code

By popular demand we have formed a dress code committee to

review what is appropriate for our employees to wear. Many complaints have come in from middle-aged employees and managers who believe that some standards need to be defined. (Since these people are the same ones who lived through the seventies, their thoughts and considerations on appropriate wear are highly valued.)

First, there is some feeling that skirts are too short. In fairness, some employees (mostly men) do not share this concern. However, a consensus group of the people mentioned above (nine women) feel that they are definitely not appropriate in our work environment. Our staff composed of five men will give this further study. It may take, however, six to eighteen months to get a significant sample, but we have asked them to report back as soon as practicable.

The committee notes with some concern that people are changing hair color with some frequency. This has caused some serious identification problems for our customers and security people. As a matter of policy, we request that employees not change color or distribution of hair. For example, if your hair is purple and spiked, keep it that way. If you have no hair, be consistent.

There has been a request for rulings on rings hanging from ears and noses. These are permissible only if they hang one eighth of an inch or less from the part of the body they are attached to. (The one eighth of an inch ruling meets the safety standards of OSHA.)

Finally the committee has been asked to rule on dress-down day. Apparently some people are wearing clothes and moccasins not appropriate for business wear. The committee, however, has ruled that Fridays will continue to be dress down days. Coincident with this the work week has been changed. All employees will work ten hours a day Monday through Thursday.

Any other concerns you may have should be sent directly to the Dress Code Committee. We will address these questions with equal dedication.

Memo Subject: New Employment Practices

In keeping with the recommendations of managers in the line departments, we are pleased to announce a new procedure for hiring people in the organization.

We will no longer hire people who appear to be in love. Recent studies show that giving orders and instructions to people who are in love is less than fruitful. Two-way communications are virtually impossible.

Applicants who respond to open questions like what, when, where, why, and how with a hum, a nod, an aimless smile, and/or frequent requests to repeat the question will not be hired.

Since this state of mind is often temporary, people in an apparent state of love may resubmit their applications in six months. Certain changes in status, such as marriage, may be up-front evidence that the problem no longer exists.

Memo Subject: Communications

It has come to the attention of this office that certain practices of marketing appear under certain conditions to have created some comment upon these, and perhaps upon others, although as far as the latter is concerned, this has not yet been verified.

However, as a means of clarifying the situation, it is desired that all employees desist immediately from the practices mentioned, except in the cases where these appear necessary, or possibly desirable, with the understanding that while prior approval is always to be recommended, it must be realized by responsible employees and supervisory personnel that such may be the case, and where this is shown, no action is to be taken.

In cases where action is indicated, responsible individuals are strictly enjoined to require compliance with corporate office memorandum dated November 25, subject "Communications," which directs that all those who have not done so will do so immediately, those that have done so will redo under the new format, and that all those who have two issues will turn in one. This will be the new policy.

Memo Subject: Coffee and Coffee Break Policies

It is apparent that we should clarify our policies with regard to coffee-breaks, but first perhaps a little background would be in order.

There have been some discussions about the pros and cons of coffee. First of all, it is a myth that coffee is harmful. It is only a problem if you have a nervous stomach, have not had breakfast, slept poorly the night before, or had an unpleasant experience driving to work. There is some evidence that excessive coffee affects memory, although no one on the staff can remember the source of this information.

We have determined recently that there are some strange bugs in the bags of coffee beans we are receiving. We have done everything possible to filter them out prior to grinding the beans. The state health inspector suggests that if some get through this probably isn't harmful. In fact it could add some protein to the beverage.

We do suggest that you not pour coffee into the potted plants in the cafeteria as has been done in the past. It is too expensive to replace them. Cafeteria people no long pour the main coffee grounds into the plumbing system because of the corrosion effect. Our sewer connections have been replaced several times.

On a similar matter, our coffee machines will be taken out of service two at a time for the next month for power scraping.

In the interest of making our cafeteria a profit center, we are asking that personnel not bring coffee to work in vacuum bottles. If this practice persists we will have to arrange a fee for sitting in the cafeteria and not buying company coffee. As you are aware, coffee cannot be consumed any other place in the building.

With this as background you are reminded that coffee breaks can only be fifteen minutes in duration. Assuming that it takes two minutes to get to the cafeteria and two minutes to get back to work, that allows eleven minutes to drink the coffee. If the coffee is too hot to drink in that time you may wish to pour out part of the coffee (again not in the plants) and fill with water.

Memo Subject: Rest Room Reengineering

We are facing a crisis in some of our headquarters facilities necessitating adjustments in policy.

First of all, you should understand that the number of rest room stalls and urinals are engineered on the basis of frequency of use and the amount of time spent at these facilities. (The amount of time spent is often expressed in an engineering usage term called holding time.) The busy hour of usage for most rest rooms is between ten and eleven in the morning,

Since we are now at the point of reengineering our rest rooms to make room for one additional work cubicle in each facility, we will be reducing the number of stalls and urinals available. (For your information this new work cubicle will be insulated to prevent distractions such as flushing.)

This change could be difficult in view of our aging work population and the increased coffee consumption per employee caused by the excessive marketing of exotic coffees. Although aging employees may be only a temporary situation in view of early retirement possibilities, the overall problem will remain.

As an interim measure all sales people and engineers on the road will be asked to use facilities in field locations. In the head-quarters building no coffee will be served at the company cafe-teria or espresso bar between the hours of 9:30 A.M. and 10:45 A.M. This should spread things out a bit.

Bringing reading material into the rest rooms will, at this point, not be prohibited but will be strongly discouraged. Live monitors will supervise this transition and make periodic reports to higher management.

Memo Subject: Suggestions for Expense Control

As most of you are aware we are facing the need for expense control, primarily because of global competition. With this in mind our auditing committee has come up with a sterling list of ideas for cutting expenses and helping us be competitive.

They are as follows:

1. Return pens. Audits of expenditures for pens reveal that there are approximately sixty-eight pens per employee, yet thousands are on order. We believe that employees are accidentally taking home pens and forgetting to bring them back. This is not to dis-courage people from doing work at home, but more than one pen at home is against company policy.

2. One hole puncher will be provided for every three employees. Three hole punched paper is cost prohibitive.

3. At the same time you bring any pictures or other graffiti to post on your cubicle walls also bring your own thumb tacks and nails. (This was a major expense during the past year.)

4. We want to applaud your use of sticky notes. However, we can save money here as well by reusing them, applying glue when appropriate.

5. Paint color in all offices will be a corporate beige from this point forward. We get a much better price when we buy paint by the carload.

6. Pulleys will be used in all offices to pass notes back and forth. This will cut down on the excessive use of e-mail.

7. Pencil extenders are being introduced to make maximum use of pencils. At the same time we will earn environmental recognition for not throwing away excessive lead.

Your expense control committee will continue to look for ways to make us world class.

Appendix B

Acronyms

These are not the only explanations for these mysterious combinations of letters we call acronyms. Your explanations are even better.

AFS   ADVOCATE FUNNY SIGNS

CAP   CATCH A PILOT

EFT   ENDURE FAILURE TEMPERAMENTALLY

AP   ADMIT PROBLEMS

FEAR   FEWER EMPLOYEES ARE REQUIRED

FIOR   FISH IN OUR RESERVOIR

ASAP   ALL SUPERVISORS ARE PATIENT

PDQ   PLEASE DON'T QUOTE

TYFSK   THANK YOU FOR SHARING KNOWLEDGE

ETA   EVERY TRIP ABANDONED

CRT   CAN'T REACH TELEPHONE

MOM   MILITIA OF MONTANA

SNAFU   SURE NOT A FUN UNDERTAKING

VDT   VODKA DEMANDS TONIC

FOB   FIND OUR BANK

TOAT   TROUBLE OVER AT TERMINAL

PIC   PHILANDER IN CLOSET

MAI   MARTINIS ARE IN

APAR   ALL POLITICIANS ARE REACHABLE

PEDS   PLAIN EVERY DAY SHOES

IPR   I PLANT RHUBARB

FTE   FIND THE ENEMY

PDO   PRETTY DARN OBVIOUS

PDI   PLEASE DON'T INQUIRE

TQC   THE QUEEN CONTROLS

PIG   PYTHON IN GRASS

DOS   DEMONSTRATEABLY OBSCURE SYSTEM

RFQ   RESERVED FOR QUACKS

EEOC   EXTRA EDICTS ON CHOICES

CPM   CAN'T PLACE MEMORY

RFP   ROUGH FOR PEOPLE

PC   PATCH CORD

FCC   FEDERAL COMMISSION CHOKES

SEC   SEARCH EVERY CLOSET

RFQ   REASONS FOR QUITTING

CAP   CERTAINLY ARE PROMPT

CEO   CHANGE EVERY ORDER

PYA   PROTECT YOUR ASSAILABLES

TGIF   THE GROUND IS FRAGILE

SOL   SAME OLD LUCK

HAP   HUG A PONY

TLC   THE LAZY COW

SOB	SAME OLD BOSS
SOP	SHARE OUR PIZZA
FYI	FORGET YOUR INHIBITIONS
TQM	THOROUGHLY QUESTIONABLE MANAGEMENT

Walls

Wall I	Wall II	Off the Wall
Production	The Boss is Coming	Just in Time
In Basket	Bulletin Board	Shred it All
Health	No Smoking	Freeze Outside
Fax	Copy	Spotted Owl
Communicate	Two way	My way
Inspire	Motivate	Restructure
Boss	Supervisor	Parent
Computers	Yes/No	Unforgiving
See No Evil	Hear No Evil	Not drug free
Lie	Cover	Spin
Elastic	Belt	Insecurity
Constant	Steady	Boring
Auditor	IRS	There to Help
Memos	Bureaucracy	Junk Mail
Constant Improvement	Standardization	Wrong Product
Shallow	Lack of Depth	Corporate Waste Basket

Management by Objective	Management by Excellence	Management by Best Seller
Whole Nine Yards	Expand	Twenty-seven Feet
Work Hard	Play Hard	Total Collapse
Conference	Meeting	Caffeine
Briefs	Skirt Suits	Female Attorney
Collar/tie	Choke	Management
Foxes	Fixes	Litigation
Tires	Cement	Rubber Meets the Road
Inter-regional	Inter-company	Interference

Lists

List I	List II	Listless
Pitch	Strike	Hard Ball
Brokers	Editors	Use of Margin
Authoritarian	Dictator	Just Do It
Communication	Restricted	Door Closed
Straining	Training	Hemorrhoids
Promotion	Sales Contest	Sunburn in Hawaii
Boating	Ocean	Level Playing Field
Intellectual	Pedantic	Senseless
Analytical	Rational	Advertising Misfit

Organization	Structure	De-layered
Crest	Wave	Beached
Shiftless	Lazy	The Other Shift
Perspective	Supervision	Good Eyes
Inventory	Cost Containment	Bludgeon the Supplier
Labor	Relations	In-laws in Waiting Room
Hackles	Temper	Shackled
Office	Plant	Withers
Ponderous	Commuting	Train of Thought

Tom Swifties in the Workplace

"I'M GLAD THAT THE COPY MACHINE IS WORKING AGAIN," SHE SAID REPEATEDLY.

"INDISCRIMINATE DRILLING FOR OIL CAN BE DISASTROUS," THE ENVIRONMENTALIST SAID CRUDELY.

"THE FULL DISCLOSURE OF INFORMATION IS IMPERFECT IN THIS CASE," THE ATTORNEY SAID BRIEFLY.

"EMPLOYEES WHO DON'T WORK SHOULD BE RELEASED," THE SUPERVISOR SAID CUTTINGLY.

"THIS PATIENT HAS MADE LITTLE PROGRESS," THE NURSE SAID CRITICALLY.

"SHE IS A WELCOME ADDITION TO THE OFFICE BUT NOT FOR THE REASON YOUR THINKING," THE MANAGER SAID ACUTELY.

"YOU'RE JUST CAN'T BUY LOYALTY ANY MORE" THE UNION NEGOTIATOR SAID STRIKINGLY.

"Giving the shirt off your back can lead to other problems," the non-giver said coldly. "Particularly if it's a blouse," she said upliftingly.

"In fact, our departments don't see eye to eye on anything," the director said blindly.

"Many persons come to work in a variety of shoe wear," the supervisor observed sneakily.

"I will not do it the way the boss wants me to," the employee said resignedly.

"The mommy track is a concept that should be rejected roundly," said the Vice President of personnel.

"Many job reclassifications will be redone," said the Human Resources manager degradingly.

"I have no idea how the theft took place," the security guard said cluelessly.

"All criminals will probably find their way to hell," the warden said condescendingly.

"I think I'll take this to a higher court," the attorney said appealingly.

"There's no excuse for writing like that," the author said cursively.

"When I'm away from work I feel guilty," the worker said absently.

"I am not sure that Maslow's theory applies," the psychologist said needlessly.

"You say the computer has a virus?" the operator asked clinically.

"I would just as soon that no one knew about this computer problem," she said mousily.

"The boss has a boiling point," the secretary said heatedly.

"If I were you I wouldn't let that get out," the security person said guardedly.

"Don't worry about those bonds falling," the broker said interestingly.

"I have an opinion on that," the newscaster said editorially.

"I think we should follow the letter of the law," the judge said strictly.

"I question whether the bridge will hold up," the engineer said civilly.

"We have too much scrap," the supervisor said rejectedly.

"We must get guns off the street," the police chief said disarmingly.

"I hate to part with this desk," the executive said movingly.

"Can we find out who wrote this?" the publisher asked anonymously.

"Where were you when the earthquake hit?" the seismologist asked unevenly.

"A portion of the cemetery will have to be sold," the planner said gravely.

"Getting a big bonus is as easy as leading lambs to slaughter," the CEO said sheepishly.

Gender Re-dress

Advance Man	One Who Makes Advances
Foreman	Jury Chair
Clothes Make the Man	Dressed for Success
Fall Guy	Accident Prone
Dirty Old Man	Unclean
Father Figure	Well Figured
Fisherman	Fish Person (fish spouse?)
Give the Devil his Due	Give the Devil its Due
Grandfather Clause	Grandparents Rights
Lumber Jack	Planer Jane
Man on the Street	Woman on the Street (8 A.M. to 5 P.M. only)
Traveling Salesman	Well-heeled Sales Person
Yes Man	Actively Affirmative
Let her Rip	Let it Rip
Handy Man	Well Equipped People
Draftsman	Window Openers

Aikido

Your hair is too long.	I didn't have any at birth.
Can't you move a little faster?	My skate board needs grease.
Are you serious?	Sometimes I'm parallel.
Are you kidding?	You want my goat?
They will never buy that.	What if they win the lottery?
Your skirt is too short.	No. My legs are too long.
Why didn't you think about it before you did it?	The fax came from headquarters.
Don't you understand plain English?	We spoke plateau in our high school.
Didn't you take the message?	I was too busy writing it down.
How many times have I told you to save what you've written on the computer?	It escapes me.
(Power at the copy machine.) How long will you be?	About 5'8"
Nice going. This customer is going to be mad.	They really are mad about our stuff.
In the old days people worked.	We were all younger then.
It happened on your shift.	I think we were in low gear.
Why can't you be logical?	Didn't I do that last week?
You're not suggesting that we do that, are you ?	Of course not. But would you tell the boss. It's his idea.

The Very Good Thing About

Junk Mail	They aren't bills.
Competitors	They provide career paths for people you let go.
Company Policies	They provide gainful employment for staff people.
Puddles	You can slosh through these when you feel childlike.
E Mail	It will force people to read at a third-grade level.
New Programs	You can unlearn the previous programs.
Giraffes	They are not afraid to stick their necks out.
Instructions for VCRs and Computer Programs	With a change in labor laws they can be delegated to children.
Bosses	You don't have to live with them.
Public Affairs	The press usually finds out about them.
People in the Plant	They get the work done (over time).
People in the Office	They brake for coffee.
The year 2008	Gurus will no longer talk about the new millennium.
Laptop Computers	They discourage cats.
Joint Ventures	You will be able to share time in jail.
Tension	It provides employment at pharmaceutical companies.
Stress	If we had any more of it our buildings would cave in.

Stiff Joints	They allow you to jog without thinking about your bad back.
Students	They too will pass.
Forepersons	They have replaced foremen.
Supervisors	They too will retire.
New Employees	They don't know when you're making mistakes.
Corporate Cultures	They change as frequently as top management.
Consultants	They make a good living from the ideas of the employees they interview.
Mainframes	You don't have to carry them.
Internet	Graffiti lives electronically.
Panic	You don't have time for a second opinion.
Urgency	(See weak bladders.)
Stupid Questions	You can respond with "No question is stupid."
Glass Ceilings	It seems transparent.
Tangents	They are humor friendly.
Being Absent-minded	You cannot identify what you are missing.
Weak Bladder	You know every public rest room within five square miles.

The Answer Man

JUST DO IT. (IF YOUR HOUSE NEEDS CLEANING?)

HEMLINES ARE CHANGING. (DO YOU SUPPOSE WE COULD GET A RAISE?)

DISPOSABLE DIAPERS. (WHAT SMELLS BAD AND NEVER GOES AWAY?)

BUDGET DEFICIT. (SAME AS ABOVE.)

LIMIT BOOKS TO TEN CHAPTERS. (WHAT WILL PUBLISHERS DO TO AVOID CHAPTER 11 IN THE FUTURE?)

TO AVOID HANG-UPS. (WHY DO YOU PACK YOUR OWN PARACHUTE?)

HANGOVERS. (WHAT HAPPENS WHEN PEOPLE IN ORGANIZATIONS TIGHTEN THEIR BELTS?)

THAT'S HOW THE COOKIE CRUMBLES. (WHAT HAPPENS WHEN YOU SAVE MONEY ON INGREDIENTS?)

JUST IN TIME. (WHEN DO YOU THINK YOU WILL BE MARRIED?)

WE'RE ON A ROLL. (WHAT DO YOU THINK ABOUT RESTRICTING THE AMOUNT OF TOILET TISSUE PER PERSON?)

Buzz Words and Clichés

State of the Art	Rhode Island
Pro-Active	Lady on the Street
Level Playing Field	Parking Lot
Mommy Track	A Running Track for Pregnant Women
Quality Circles	Chocolate Covered Doughnuts
What Goes Around Comes Around	Quality Circles
The Whole Nine Yards	A Sub-division With Nine Houses

Worst Case Scenario	All Eggs are Broken
Zero Defect	An Imperfect Zero
Sliding Scale	One That Gives a Higher Weight Everyday
Co-dependent	People who Share Debt
Brainstorm	Cloudy Eyes
Burnout	A Four Alarm Fire
Time Management	The Supervisor in Charge of Winding the Clock
Back to Basics	Fire the Sales Manager
If Your Cup Runneth Over	Male: Tip the Mug; Female: Go on a Diet

Definitions

Fax	A machine that eliminates personal contact.
Big Blue	Pacific Ocean
GM	Generally mobile
Downscaling	Do, ti, la, so, fa, mi, re, do
Reengineering	One more look at stress
PC	Planned Confusion
Overhead	Our overseer
Desktop	What one finds under corporate paper
Critical Path	(1) Where my spouse scolded me; (2) the hallway to the building rest rooms

Computer Definitions

RAM	Regrets are Mandatory
ROM	Remember Our Mom
Orphans	Mother Board Problems
Full Mouse Support	Works faster, however, when hungry
Pop-Up Utilities	Short explosive sound with a power outage
On Line	No Hang-ups
Spreadsheet	Electronic blankie for bean counters
Shared Interface	Co-dependent equipment
Multi-boot	Criticism from both boss and staff
Windows	The need for closure
User Friendly	A boss that smiles

Bibliography

Adams, James L. Conceptual Blockbusting, Menlo Park: Addison Wesley 1986

Adams, Scott, The Dilbert Principle, New York: Harper Collins, 1996

Adams, Scott, Dogbert's Top Secret Management Handbook. New York: Harper Collins, 1996

Barreca, Regina, They Used To Call Me Snow White...but I Drifted, New York, Viking, 1991

Blumenfeld, Esther and Alpern, Lynne Humor at Work, Atlanta, Peachtree 1994

Cousins, Norman, The Anatomy of an Illness, New York: Bantam, 1983

Cousins, Norman, Head First, New York: Penguin, 1990

Goodman, Joel, Laughing Matters, (magazine), Saratoga Springs, NY: The Humor Project, 1996

Helitzer, Melvin, Comedy Writing Secrets, Cincinnati: Writer's Digest, 1992

Klein, Allen, The Healing Power of Humor, New York: Putnam, 1989

Kushner, Malcolm The Light Touch, New York: Simon and Schuster, 1990

Mead, Shepherd How To Succeed In Business Without Really Trying, New York: Simon and Schuster 1958

Paulson, Terry L., Making Humor Work, Los Altos, Ca.: Crisp, 1989

Perret, Gene, Comedy Writing Step by Step, New York: Samuel French, 1990

Peter, Laurence and Dana, Bill, The Laughter Prescription, New York: Ballantine, 1982

Peters, Tom, Thriving on Chaos, New York: Knopf, 1987

Peters, Tom, The Pursuit of WOW, New York: Vintage, 1994

Ruggiero, Vincent Ryan, The Art of Thinking, New York: Harper Collins, 1995

von Oech, Roger, A Kick in the Seat of the Pants, New York: Harper & Row, 1986

Permission Acknowledgments

Grateful acknowledgment is made to the following for permission to reprint previously published material.

Addison-Wesley Publishing Company Inc., *Conceptual Blockbusting*, Third Edition. Copyright 1986 by James L. Adams. Reprinted with permission.

Doubleday, a division of Bantam Doubleday Dell Publishing Group, Inc. Sam Walton, *Made in America* by Sam Walton with John Huey, 1993. Reprinted with permission.

Fortune Magazine (c) 1994 Time Inc. All rights reserved. "Is Herb Kelleher America's Best CEO," by Kenneth Labich. Reprinted by permission.

HR Magazine, "Building Fun in Your Organization" by David J. Abramis. Reprinted with the permission of HR Magazine published by the Society for Human Resource Management, Alexandria, Virginia.

IMG Literary, Copyright 1989 by Norman Cousins, "Norman Cousins Helps Other Patients as He Once Helped Himself—by Laughing," *Good Housekeeping Magazine*. Reprinted by permission of IMG Literary.

Alfred A. Knopf, New York, 1987. Thriving on Chaos by Tom Peters. Reprinted by permission.

LAUGHING MATTERS magazine edited by Joel Goodman and published by THE HUMOR Project, Inc., 110 Spring Street, Saratoga Springs, NY 12866 (518 587 8770). Reprinted by permission of the author.

New York Times, Personal Health column by Jane E. Brody, New York Times, (c) Copyright by The New York Times Co. Reprinted by permission.

Simon and Schuster, How To Succeed in Business Without Really Trying by Shepherd Mead, 1958; copyright renewed (c) 1980 by Shepherd Mead. Reprinted by permission.

Statement From Steelhead Press

We absolutely guarantee that, as a result of reading this book, you will:

1. Find the real value of humor at work and/or

2. Laugh at least four times (smiles included)

If this doesn't happen we will refund your money. (Gladly and reluctantly.) You do not need to send the book back. Give it to someone as a white elephant gift, if this pleases you.

For additional copies of this book you can contact your neighborhood book store. If they don't happen to have it in stock, they tell us they will be happy to order it for you. Here's another option: You can send your check for $14.95 plus $3.00 for shipping for the first book and $1.00 shipping for each additional book.

Steelhead Press
P.O. Box 219277
Portland, OR 97225-9277

We will immediately send you a copy of the book, most likely in a brownish wrapper. (Your neighbors need not know.)